WILLIE IRVING

Terrierman, Huntsman and Lakelander

Dedication

To the memory of
the Irving brothers – true Lakelanders;
and to Maud Vickers and Pearl Wilson,
Willie's daughters, without whose
help this book would not have been possible.

Acknowledgements

I would like to thank Maud and Pearl in particular, for allowing me to write this book about such a fascinating and worthy subject. Also, my thanks go to everyone who has aided my research and provided photographs regarding the life and times of Willie Irving. The hospitality and generosity shown has been much appreciated. I would also like to express my appreciation to Mr and Mrs Gordon Bland who worked so hard in gathering on to computer memory vital information I have been able to use.

WILLIE IRVING

Terrierman, Huntsman and Lakelander

Seán Frain

MERLIN UNWIN BOOKS

Published by:
Merlin Unwin Books
Palmers House
7 Corve Street
Ludlow
Shropshire SY8 1DB
U.K.

www.merlinunwin.co.uk

Designed and set in Bembo by Merlin Unwin
Printed in England by Cromwell Press, Trowbridge

ISBN 978-1-906122-02-7

Contents

Glossary

Bay, to: This is when a terrier barks at a fox in order to bolt it, or guide the diggers. Hounds also bay, or 'give tongue' either whilst hunting a line, or marking an earth. To 'stand at bay' is when the fox turns and faces the hounds at close quarters.

Bield: or borran. A naturally formed rock-pile. This term is used exclusively in the Lake District.

Bink, to: When a fox crawls onto a narrow ledge on a steep crag in order to escape hounds, it is said 'to bink'.

Bobbery pack: A scratch hunting pack of local dogs including hounds, terriers, lurchers, sheepdogs.

Bolt, to: When a fox leaves its earth and makes for the open ground, usually after a terrier has been sent in, though foxes have been known to bolt when hounds mark and dig at an earth.

Borran: A naturally-formed rock-pile, as opposed to a man-made pile found in many old quarries. Borrans often cover a vast area and are very deep. They are incredibly dangerous places in which to enter a terrier.

Bothy: A simple mountain hut in a remote area, often stone built, offering shelter to shepherds or anyone lost overnight on the mountains and fells.

Brock: Colloquial term for a badger.

Brush: Colloquial term for the tail of a fox. These are like a bottle-brush and come in a range of colours and sizes, some with large white tips, others without. Some are even black.

Charlie: Colloquial term for a fox, thought to originate from the MP Charles James Fox. Foxes are sometimes also referred to as 'Charles James', or 'Reynard', or Tod.

Coupled: This is when terriers are shackled together using a small length of chain known as Couplings. These help keep terriers under control, preventing the risk of them sheep worrying and the possibility of a terrier sneaking off to go down a nearby earth when its owner isn't looking. Hounds are also coupled at times, especially young-sters. These are chained to older, wiser hounds (trenchers) who will help teach them manners and respect for livestock. Couplings, however, do not prevent terriers from getting into an earth and getting stuck there, so vigilance is required when coupled terriers are within reach of a fox den.

Den: The underground home of a fox – *see also* Earth.

Draw, to: When the Huntsman takes his hounds in search of a fox, they are said to 'draw' a Fellside, for example, or under crags. They run around, searching for a scent trail (a line). Huntsmen draw all the most likely places.

Earth: A fox's underground den.

Entered to fox: When a hound or terrier, on reaching maturity, is used for the hunting of foxes. Once a hound or terrier has 'served its apprenticeship' and is now working foxes, either hunting their line or going into fox earths, they are said to be entered to fox.

Fell, a: A moor, or mountain. This term is used in the Lake District, North Yorkshire and North Lancashire in particular.

Find, to: When hounds 'find' it means they have encountered the skulking/ resting fox and made it move from its hiding place. A terrier is said 'to find' when it stops running and begins baying at its fox, which is usually trapped in at this point.

Gather, to blow the: When the Huntsman blows a set series of notes on his horn to call back the hounds, this signals the end of hunting for the day. It can take some time for the hounds to return when the Gather is blown and sometimes hounds remain missing overnight if they have gone miles adrift from the pack. The Huntsman will search for missing hounds for hours, often until darkness falls.

Ghyll: Pronounced 'gill'. *See also* Gryke. A deep ravine which usually carries a mountain stream down to the valley bottom. Some ghylls are very steep and nigh-on impossible to cross.

Ground, go to: When a pursued fox no longer feels safe fleeing above ground, he heads into an earth in order to escape

the hounds. This is when the terriers take over. They are entered either solely or as a couple, in order to either bolt or kill the fox underground. The latter is particularly preferable if the fox is a lamb- or poultry-killer. It requires a great deal of skill for the terrier to kill a fox which has gone to ground. To avoid injury, the terrier has to try for a throat-hold, throttling the fox and cutting off its air supply.

Gryke: *see also* Ghyll. A gryke is a fissure or crack in the crag face or outcrop of rocks.

Huntsman: In the Fell country the Huntsman is appointed by the Hunt Committee to look after hounds and kennels, feed them, keep their environment clean and in good repair and treat minor ailments or injuries. The Huntsman is often the sole person employed, in which case his job can include the role of Kennelman, Whipper-in and terrierman. In Willie Irving's day, however, a Whipper-in was usually employed to assist the Huntsman, both while out hunting, and back at the kennels. The Huntsman is paid during the hunting season only (September to around the middle of May).

Line, a: A scent trail, or a 'drag'. When hounds suddenly get on the scent of a fox and start following it as one, instead of all fanning out, this is called hunting a line.

Made worker: Refers to a hound or terrier which is so experienced that it can be relied upon to do its job without any further training.

Master of Foxhounds (MFH): The Master oversees the running of the pack of hounds and helps the committee to organise hunting and social events, as well as liaising with farmers and landowners. This is an important, hands-on post and the MFH is heavily involved in the day-to-day running of the hunt.

Meet, a: The place where hunt staff, followers, hounds and terriers gather at the start of the day's hunting. Hospitality is usually enjoyed, with tea, coffee, whiskey and brandy often supplied before the start. Afterwards, a social evening at the same venue is sometimes held, or the night before, where drink and food such as a traditional tattie pot (a kind of stew) is enjoyed. Pub games, dancing and sing-songs are the norm. All the different hunts have their own particular songs, though some are universal such as 'Joe Bowman'.

Puppy walking: When weaned, young hounds are 'farmed out' to hunt supporters, often farmers and villagers, to be raised, socialised, and familiarised with livestock and other dogs, so that they are already well behaved when they start hunting. These hounds then go back to live with the same families when the hunting season ends each year, leaving the Huntsman and Whip to find employment elsewhere. It is a great service to the hunt, as the puppy walkers personally fund the care of the hounds while they have them.

Reynard: Term for a fox, also known as Charlie. The word Reynard is of French origin.

Run down, to: To catch a fox on open land, in other words to exhaust and out-manoeuvre it, often after a lengthy hunt.

Typey: Refers to a terrier; handsome, good-looking, of good conformation.

Whipper-in: The assistant to the Huntsman on hunting days, as well as in the general care of the hounds at the kennels. The Whip will often climb out higher than the Huntsman and watch out for a fox leaving its chosen lair as the hounds draw across a Fellside. A Whipper-in must be as fit and keen as the Huntsman and his role is just as important although few packs have the funds to employ a professional Whip these days.

Worry, to: To kill a fox by throttling and shaking it; either below ground using a terrier or above ground using the hounds.

The fox has no natural predator but man. Without hunting, there would be no incentive to tolerate, let alone preserve, any fox. Hunting gives the fox worth in the fells. The result is wholly good: a stable, tolerable population of healthy foxes managed by an exhilarating activity which is the centre of a way of life.

Submission on behalf of the Central Committee of Fell Packs to the Committee of Inquiry into Hunting with Dogs

Introduction: a Typical Fell Hunt

It was April 25th 1932 and the lowland fields and lower pastures of the fellsides, where the greens of the fields met the browns and greys of the higher and wilder mountains, were full of the bleating of newborn lambs, suckling eagerly, their woolly tails wagging furiously to and fro, to and fro. Lambing time was incredibly hard work for the hill shepherd, when his duties were seemingly endless.

Many ewes would need some help delivering their young-sters and so the shepherd was often down to his shirt sleeves, with the chilled wind nipping at his flesh, his arm inside and his fingers working to untangle twin lambs in order that they could at last reach the outside world. The shepherd would hardly go to bed at this time, grabbing as much sleep as possible dosing in a chair by the fire. Often he would have had to find a foster parent for some lamb that had been rejected by its mother, for some unknown reason. Sometimes a ewe had died whilst giving birth. Other ewes might have become distressed after delivering a stillborn, or, worse still, after losing a lamb to a marauding fox, and these were usually given one of the rejected, or orphaned, lambs to keep them content. A ewe that had difficulty with delivery could sometimes pine away and die with the absence of a youngster to give it focus and purpose, so it was impor-tant that such ewes were given an orphan to raise. They could soon recover once they had set their minds on 'child rearing'.

It was at that time that shepherds in the Crummock Water area of the Lake District began losing lambs to a marauding fox and the local hunt was called in to deal with it. This was a tradition stretching back centuries and was an almost certain way of catching up with the culprit. A fox would stalk lambs around the birthing and rearing pastures and in doing so would leave his, or her, scent behind. However, by late April all things were growing due to increased light and heat and so scent would very quickly disappear once the sun was up. So at first light, long before the sun had risen fully and was at last warming the land again, the hounds were taken around those pastures where lambs were being killed.

The scent of the fox was then discovered, if all went well, and hounds would then follow what is termed a 'drag', that is, the line the fox had taken after killing the newborn lamb. They could spend quite some time working out this drag, but usually they would find where Reynard had chosen to lie up for the day. Sometimes Reynard would eat the lamb, but very often he would bite off the head and take that alone. On occasions the fox would leave behind a fatally wounded lamb, or even several lambs, all badly bitten through the skull and left slowly to die. Any surviving the head-bite often suffered severe brain damage, even if the poor creature did eventually pull through, so shepherds would usually put such injured beasts down.

The fox, when eventually found, could be lying out in undergrowth; in deep heather, gorse, brambles, bracken, or rush beds; or maybe on the ledge of a crag, or even deep underground in what are known as 'borrans'. These are huge and deep piles of rock that have been naturally formed in ancient times and if the fox was found in such vast and difficult places they were either turned out (bolted), or finished off underground (worried) by terriers. The Lake District has been producing some of the gamest working terriers in the world for centuries. Such terriers have narrow shoulders, in order to negotiate the tight tunnels beneath rock and scree, tight, coarse jackets, in order to keep out the worst of the weather, and strong heads and jaws, for obvious reasons. Hill foxes were game quarry and knew how to handle themselves, so only the most stout of heart terrier could bolt, or worry them, in such bad country. The Fell, Lakeland and Patterdale terriers are all originally from this region of Northern England and they have been specially bred through generations in order to deal with the tough and hardy hill foxes that inhabit this region in large numbers.

On that particular April morning, while it was still dark and the majority of folk were still abed, the Huntsman selected a small pack and a few shaggy terriers accompanied them as they made their way to the lambing fields. Birdsong began to fill the air as darkness gave out to the cold light of dawn and it was then, in the half-light of a chilly spring morning, that hounds were cast close to the spot where a couple more lambs had fallen victim during the night. At last hounds began 'feathering' – casting round all over the place on a cold scent, trying to fathom which way their fox had made its exit after killing the lambs.

Some of the best of the pack began whimpering and slowly, slowly they moved forward. Although scattered at first, the pack gradually became more tightly knit as they made progress and headed across the lowland pastures, making now, though still at rather a slow pace, for the open fells. Many foxes lurk in the low country, as food is more easily come by there, but they would head back to the mountains when hounds were in pursuit, for it was there they felt safest and it was there where they could use their cunning to full effect. The hounds easily scaled the high stone walls of the pastures and soon found themselves on the slopes of Grasmoor, with our Huntsman and one or two keen locals following closely behind. The shaggy terriers milled around the Huntsman's feet and pushed and pulled all over the

Albert Thomas and Annie Irving with Tramp and Turk in the early 1930s.

place, eager for hounds to signal a find and hoping to get in among the dark passages of the crags where they felt very much at home.

Hollins was the place where lambs were being taken and by now the hounds had travelled quite a distance without a find. But suddenly, among the grey rocks and the deep heather, their whimpers and muffled bays began to swell to full cry as they had their quarry afoot and began hunting it around the high slopes of Grasmoor Fell. There were several rocky places where foxes could go to ground on this huge swell of mountain, which was often topped with mist, rain, or snow, but Reynard knew of the terriers and he wished to keep clear of them. His mind was made up. He would remain above ground and take his chances with hounds, for he hoped he could throw them off, as he had no doubt done on many occasions in the past.

He therefore took them over rock and scree, through heather where secret pathways had been worn in the undergrowth for several generations, across centuries rather than decades, and then he led them out onto the wild tops where springtime hadn't yet reached, for there were still traces of snow in places, particularly where the ground was sheltered from the sun and the temperatures remained constantly low at this time of year. In fact the fell tops all around were ribbed with the last snows of winter and the followers stopped on occasion, to look for hounds, true, but also to enjoy the magnificent, incomparable views, which changed dramatically with each turn, with each breathtaking and energy-sapping push upwards, ever upwards.

They remained on Grasmoor for quite some time and Reynard seemed reluctant to leave the mountain where he had no doubt spent much of his life. He kept ahead of hounds, but scenting conditions proved very good indeed and the pack were hunting well, so he began feeling the pressure after a while and decided it was best to leave the area. He now made for the lower slopes of Grasmoor and was eventually back in the low country, the followers descending as quickly as possible. The pack, although fleet of foot and pushing their quarry hard, were slowed by obstacles such as fences, hedges and walls. Still they pressed on, their noses questing, their bodies surging forward at each upturn of scent, their limbs slowing with each fall in quality. But still they worked, still they searched, trying to fathom where

Reynard had headed and still they came, rushing across the fields and through woodlands, past farms and over narrow country lanes, their eager chorus swelling, swelling, where scent was keenest.

Over Brackenthwaite Hows they surged, past the local quarry, where the hunt was joined by a few of the workers, and on to Corn How where, to the dismay of Huntsman and shepherd in particular, the hounds began struggling and finally lost the line altogether, despite their best efforts. Scent had been great up on the higher places, with low temperatures and damp to hold onto it, but down in the low country the air was much milder and dry and so they just couldn't hold onto and own the line any longer. It wasn't for want of trying.

At dawn two days later and yet again our Huntsman loosed his pack in low-lying land where more lambs had perished and again they hunted a fox, no doubt the same one, on Grasmoor. But again Reynard managed to evade capture by keeping above ground and running hounds off as scent faded with the rising sun. No lamb casualties that night, but on the following night, April 28th 1932, the same shepherd lost even more stock and the hounds were called to try again.

On April 29th hounds were loosed near the lambing fields and they hit off a drag, which unmistakably belonged to the guilty party. They stuck to the cold line and eventually were rewarded, as they roused their fox not far from Hollins, at Cold Ghyll, near the current site of the hunt kennels. The music of the pack filled the morning air, drowning out the early spring birdsong and filling hearts with joy and anticipation. Over the past few days the Huntsman had grown increasingly frustrated at not being able to account for this lamb-worrying fox and he fully intended to catch up with it today. He was determined not to leave the fells until this fox had been well and truly stopped in its tracks.

Scent was good and the pack were now in full cry, leaving their Huntsman and a few followers struggling to keep up. The fox took them around Gasgale (pronounced 'Gaskell') Crags, over rough, steep ground to Gasgale Ghyll and then on to the wild country of Dove Crags, an intimidating spot at any time of year, but particularly so during the chill of winter when the winds there could blow a full-grown man off his feet. The fox now made for Coledale (pronounced 'Caudale') and away past Hobcarton Crags, over high and rough country to Hobcarton itself, in the direction of Whinlatter Pass and the huge woodlands there. However, just before the woods he turned, pushed by the relentless pack, and doubled back across open and rough country for the higher slopes of Whiteside.

Still the fox was reluctant to go to ground; probably his past experience told him to keep in the open, but he was so hard-pressed that he descended and once again found himself in the low country, among fields and farms at Lanthwaite Green, not too far from where he had been stealing the lambs. No doubt his intention was to throw the hounds off here, for he knew that scent would be poorer where temperatures had risen. However, although this trick had worked for him before, it failed on this occasion and the pressing hounds soon persuaded him to make for higher ground once more. En route they chivvied him around fields and woodland and gave him no rest, until once again he was on rough ground, with the baying, fast-paced pack close behind.

He climbed the steep-sided mountains of Whin Ben, Brack-enthwaite and Grasmoor and just made Dove Crags where he leapt up onto a narrow ledge and 'binked' there, which basically means that he lay down, refusing to move, knowing that hounds couldn't reach him. However, a terrier could and one was soon heading towards the skulking fox. The terrier, gripping the slippery grey rock, bayed and lunged at the quarry. Reynard was forced to move once more and bolted from the ledge at surprising speed, negotiating the deadly crag with the agility of a cat. Hounds were once again quickly in pursuit and were soon pressing their quarry hard indeed. So hard, in fact, that he was forced to make for a rocky spot on the face of Grasmoor where he at last went to ground, reluctant to face the hounds any longer.

Foxes are often bolted, which means forced to resurface and then the hunt continues above ground, where Reynard has a better chance of escape. However, this was a lamb-killer they were after, one which had taken quite a heavy toll of stock, so the Huntsman was keen that this particular fox be accounted for as quickly as possible. And so he put into the rocky crevice two of his best terriers, Tramp and Rex, in the hope that they would find and worry their quarry below ground. A single terrier can struggle to pin down a fox inside a large rocky fortress, so the fact that two terriers were entered tells us that this was a big place.

Tramp and Rex soon found where their quarry had hidden itself, their loud baying informing those above ground of this fact. Sure enough, the two pinned down their foe and they set about worrying it below, while the Huntsman and followers dug down in the area of the sound, shifting soil and rock until eventually, after much graft they uncovered the two terriers. The culprit was a large, quite elderly, dog fox. The Huntsman opened up his gut on the spot and sure enough, discovered there a belly full of lamb, confirming that this was indeed the fox preying on the lambing fields and the one they had hunted, without success, on at least two previous occasions. The important thing was that a lamb-worrying fox had been accounted for and his campaign of slaughter put to an end. The Huntsman returned hounds and terriers to the kennels with a great feeling of accomplishment, leaving behind a happy shepherd and a much more secure flock of sheep.

Our Huntsman was Willie Irving, the subject of this book, and the pack was the famous and historical Melbreak Foxhounds, which remain in this part of the Lakes to this day. Willie was one of the most popular, efficient and successful of Huntsmen to have led this pack, or any pack for that matter, but he was much more than just a fell pack Huntsman. He was also a famous Lakeland terrier breeder who helped found and shape the breed. Another claim to fame was as a very successful fell runner. Later in life he worked for the Hound Trailing Association (HTA) and helped establish this sport across Britain and Ireland, where he made many friends. Willie lived life to the full and left behind him a legacy, which as you will see, is well worth a book!

He was a living legend and much mystery has surrounded him since his death, particularly regarding his exploits as Huntsman and Terrierman to the Melbreak pack. This book aims to establish facts and dispel myths, though we will in no way learn everything about the man who was Willie Irving.

He was a prominent member of the Lakeland Terrier Association (LTA) and was close friends with some of the best hunters and terrier breeders the north has ever produced. Best of all, he left us valuable records of almost every hunt he took part in with his famous 'Laal' Melbreak, including much of the terrier work which will be of great interest to all who admire our working breeds of earth dog. Threaded throughout this book are true accounts based on these diaries and newspaper articles published at the time, as well as the memories of Maud and Pearl (Willie's daughters) and other hunt followers. I recommend the reader purchase the OL4 Ordnance Survey map covering the North-western area of the Lakes, country through which it is possible to follow every hunt discussed in great detail.

A 19th century photograph of the Irvings at Wath Farm, Ennerdale

CHAPTER 1

Born into a Tradition

The family name of Irving is originally of Irish origin, but the clan settled in Scotland centuries ago and legends have sprung up as to how they eventually arrived and settled in the English county of Cumberland. One legend says that the early members of the Irving family were driven out of Scotland because of religious persecution. Another says that they were forced to leave because they were criminal sheep rustlers. Few families would be proud of that label, but it has to be remembered that both sheep and cattle rustling were common practice in Scotland, usually fuelled by poverty. Many Scottish Lairds employed 'ruffians' such as Rob Roy to guard their livestock from such practices. Such family tales must not be taken too seriously: what is certain is that the Irvings have long come from farming stock and it was to farming that Willie Irving was born. His grandparents ran a mixed farm of sheep, cattle and horses in the Ennerdale district at Wath (pronounced 'Woth') Farm.

The Lake District has long been a livestock-rearing county and because of this there is a deeply entrenched tradition of hunting any predators that leave enough scent for hounds and terriers to follow. Bounties, sometimes large ones, were paid for each predator carcass, or maybe just a tail, that was presented to the local church warden. This attracted professional hunters into the area, particularly during the sixteenth, seventeenth and eighteenth centuries. The Irving family has held a deep interest in hounds and terriers for generations and it is just possible that an Irving of earlier times settled in the Lakes for this very reason. Economic hardship, even persecution may well have been the reason for the family leaving Scotland in the first place, but the large bounties paid in the fell country may be what kept them in this area. A good living could once be made if pest control was carried out in conjunction with farming.

Hunting and farming are inextricably linked throughout the Lake District. Until recently almost every farm had among its livestock a hound or two, alongside a brace or so of rough and ready terriers. Farmers, if losing livestock, would then come together and have an informal hunt with a pack of sometimes rather unruly hounds (a bobbery pack). Very often their quarry would be run to ground, be dug out using terriers and swiftly accounted for. The cash bounty would then be claimed and no doubt shared among the farmers of the district, for the funds raised would be quite considerable over the year. These funds were also used to help keep hounds at that time, as there were a few packs in kennels and not all were trencher-fed (put out with families). This is probably the kind of spontaneous early hunting that prevailed when the Irving family first settled in Cumberland.

Scotland and Wales dealt with problems from predators in a similar way and there is an interesting account in Jane Ridley's superb book, *Fox Hunting*, which tells us much about how the hill farmers handled a lamb-killer. This particular account concerns Cardiganshire in Wales, with the Gogerddan hounds. A farmer had lost several young lambs and the predator left a distinctive mark on each victim from what appeared to be a broken tooth. As usual, the fox had made its attacks down in the low country and so a drag was hit around the pastures at first light. The trail took the pack onto the hill, with a hard frost making the going difficult. However, hounds stuck to their task, hunting the fox down for hours on the hill before finally running it to ground by late afternoon.

A terrier was put in, but they didn't want their quarry bolted in case it escaped, so digging commenced at 3:30pm and went on by the light of lanterns well into the evening, the quarry finally being dug-out at 7:30pm. The fox had indeed got a broken tooth, which confirmed that this was the culprit. Such effective hunting exploits were repeated thousands of times over throughout Scotland, Wales and the fell country of Northern England: and this was the same hunting tradition into which Willie Irving was introduced during his formative years.

He was named after his father William Irving, despite not being the eldest son. John Tyson Irving was the eldest brother and he was so named because William had married into the Tyson family who were a famous and prominent hunting clan in the western fells. They farmed around the Ennerdale district and Willie's daughter Maud is pretty certain the Tysons lived at Cald Fell. She can remember her father telling her about the farm there, where he spent much of his time during his school holidays.

Willie Tyson was a well-known breeder of working fell terriers during the days of Tommy Dobson. Willie Porter's terriers were descended from Tyson stock. Will Ritson bred similar terriers, having undoubtedly got his initial stock from Tyson, which he used when he was Huntsman to the old Ennerdale pack, before they amalgamated

Willie Irving senior.

with the Eskdale in 1895. Willie Tyson was no doubt of the same blood as Sarah, William Irving's bride, and this may well be from where the young Willie inherited his passion for terriers – a passion that would be with him throughout his long and eventful life. It is interesting to note that Willie Tyson of Ennerdale, unlike many breeders of his day, aimed to produce very hard coated terriers which could stand up to the harsh conditions of a Lake District winter.

Terrier's coats during the nineteenth and early twentieth centuries were rather poor to say the least – open, lank and long. A Bedlington's coat gave little protection from wet and icy winds - the worst killers of terriers exposed to the high country. Tyson succeeded in producing what became known as typical Patterdale terriers that

LEFT: *Mrs Sarah Irving, formerly Tyson (far left), Willie Irving's mother.*
ABOVE: *Annie Irving, Willie's little sister.*

could both finish a fox among the rocks far below ground, and stand up to hours of hunting on the fells during the most severe of weather conditions. But why are Tyson's Patterdale terriers of interest to us? The reader will learn exactly why as we progress through the book, but I must not run ahead of my tale!

William Irving (junior) was born on August 6th 1898 at Ennerdale. William (senior) and Sarah had their first child, John Tyson Irving on March 10th 1897 and it seems that a farm later became available in the south. With sons to consider, William senior may have had ambitions to take up a more prosperous business in a more fertile place and the family decided to move south. Willie was three years old when the family moved to Northamptonshire in 1901, with Annie Irving being born in 1902. Possibly he and Sarah were missing family and friends in the Lake District or maybe things hadn't worked out in Northamptonshire, but for whatever reason, William and Sarah decided to head back up north and had settled in the western Lakes again by 1905 when Henry Irving was born on April 17th. Then came Arthur Edward Irving on February 4th 1907. Maud is certain that the family moved to Bankhouse Farm near Ennerdale sometime before 1906. In that year William senior joined the Ennerdale show committee, undoubtedly a sign that he was a successful man in the district by now. Willie, along with his four siblings, was born into a life of Lakeland tradition and the Irving family were popular and deeply involved in the community.

Willie grew up surrounded by hounds and terriers, living in an area hunted by the Eskdale and Ennerdale hounds, as well as the Melbreak pack, and the West Cumberland Otterhounds which were hunted at that time by 'Doggy' Robinson. Also, the Egremont Otterhounds hunted in the same area, as did smaller private packs fielded by farmers and villagers alike and often consisting of hounds, terriers, farm collies and street curs. Beagles also played an important part in Willie's schoolboy days and he continued to follow them as much as possible throughout his life. The Long family of Egremont often got together with other enthusiasts and they fielded bobbery packs that hunted anything which left a trail of scent. They enjoyed good hunts every Sunday, almost every month of the year, so Willie had plenty of opportunities to work with dogs, learning much about them even as a small child. It is also likely that his parents walked hounds for either the Melbreak, or the Eskdale and Ennerdale, possibly even both packs, during Willie's youth and no doubt the young lad helped care for them. These early lessons with hounds would stand him in good stead when he entered professional hunt service during his twenties.

Willie grew up with his brothers steeped in a tradition of farming and fell hunting and it is no wonder that such a love of hounds and terriers could be found throughout the family. His elder brother (John) Tyson Irving grew up to become a farmer, following a family tradition, while both Willie and Arthur, the youngest brother, would enter professional hunt service. Arthur whipped-in at the Blencathra for two seasons (1937-39), before finally becoming Huntsman at the Eskdale and Ennerdale Foxhounds, under the Masterships of both Willie and Jack Porter. Brother Henry (known as Harry) Irving also had a keen interest in hunting and he bred some very useful and typey Lakeland terriers. He was also one-time secretary of the Eskdale and Ennerdale Foxhounds. So hunting played a very important part in the life of the Irving family and both the Eskdale and Ennerdale, and Melbreak, packs were followed when Willie was 'nowt but a wee nipper'.

His childhood days were spent at Ennerdale school and it was here that he developed a love of sport, particularly Association Football and what were then known as Guide Races. Willie was a fit, athletic young lad and he was soon proving to be very active indeed, filling his time with all manner of different interests, including a love of the fell country, its flora and fauna. This love of the natural world remained with him throughout his life and Maud and Pearl, his two children, have fond memories of days spent out on the fells, or in the fields, enjoying wild flowers and wildlife. On several occasions Willie would take his daughters to see litters of fox cubs playing outside their dens, while sternly instructing them not to tell anyone of the whereabouts of such cubs.

In those days cubs were often dug out, raised and then sold, often for the sake of restocking a hunt country that had been depleted by diseases such as mange, or distemper, or possibly over-shooting by keepers. Many country periodicals carried advertisements for foxes for sale. Finding, digging out and selling cubs could be quite a prosperous sideline for anyone who was in need of a spare few quid. Also, farmers, especially shepherds, were very uncomfortable with the thoughts of cubs being raised on, or near, their land, so they were not averse to having them dug out and destroyed, or removed. One can understand why. A vixen with a hungry family to raise

could often turn to lamb killing or poultry worrying and this could be an expensive loss to any landowner, or tenant farmer – hence the reason for Willie swearing his children to secrecy regarding the whereabouts of a litter. He knew they wouldn't last long if discovered and wished to protect them from unnecessary disturbance.

Like most countrymen Willie was passionate about the natural cycle and wouldn't dream of taking a litter of cubs for no good reason. If a vixen from one of the litters he knew about was killing lambs, then he wouldn't hesitate to act in order to protect the farmer's interests and the guilty fox would be hunted and taken, whenever possible, along with her youngsters. Otherwise he left them strictly alone and allowed

Arthur Irving with his terriers which were sired by Copper Coin.

nature to replenish the land after winter had taken its heavy toll. He was certainly a good example for any who hunt foxes today. There are reports of guns being used all year round in most areas and this is bad for the fox population. A summer off-season *must* be observed, except, of course, where livestock is being worried. Even then it is important to try to exterminate only the guilty party, though innocent foxes are bound to be shot when hounds are not being used in the traditional Lakeland method of drawing around lambing fields.

Willie certainly seems to have made the most of his school days and holidays were spent hunting, helping out on family farms, or enjoying sheep dog trials, guide races and hound-trailing. This keen interest was obviously in the blood from both sides of the family: the Tysons and the Irvings, so Willie grew up with a love of farming which, as we shall see, stood him in good stead for the days ahead when he would become a professional hunt servant. As a lad he would help see to the horses, as these were still used around the farm at that time for ploughing, spreading, harrowing, seeding and all kinds of essential tasks. He would no doubt help out at milking time and mucking out time too, as well as carrying out work among the sheep. Springtime holidays such as Easter would be spent assisting with lambing and no doubt the long summer holidays were taken up mainly with helping gather in hay and crops, or enjoying the spectacle of trials, hound-trailing and guide races. Winter holidays were spent following hounds on as many occasions as was possible.

1926/27 SEASON

Willie started as Huntsman of the Melbreak hounds on **September 11th** 1926 at the age of 28, with 28 hounds making up the pack, 10 of which were puppies. His first hunt was at Low Fell on that date, but he wasn't successful until the **15th** of that same month. This date marks the occasion when Willie Irving accounted for his first fox with the Melbreak Foxhounds. The meet was likely at Lorton village and hounds drew in the low country, no doubt having a fox away from Cass How Wood, or nearby Clint's Wood, hunting around the pastures and then on to Rogerscale where their fox was run to ground in a drain. It wouldn't bolt and was worried underground by the terriers before it could be dug out. Scent can be difficult during the early part of the season, but Willie had inherited a very useful pack from the previous Huntsman. As he records, they killed a fox during each of their next six outings, with a long drag taking hounds onto Grasmoor and to a rock hole there on **October 9th**. A terrier was put in and the fox was caught among the rocks and was worried by hounds.

Willie often doesn't state which terriers were used, but he had brought some good ones with him which had seen service with the Eskdale and Ennerdale pack, such as Riff and Floss. His next hunt of some note was on **October 16th** when the meet was at Lamplugh village. A fox was soon roused, almost at the first draw, and it proved a game 'un' indeed. Reynard was a formidable opponent and he headed for the fells almost immediately, taking to Lamplugh Fell and over the wild tops where the going was very difficult. Scent wasn't exactly 'screaming', but it was at least holding and the hounds were able to stick to the line. Reynard took them all over the tops here and the hunt went on and on, with hounds persisting until, an incredible six hours and thirty minutes later, they accounted for their quarry on Melbreak, the mountain that gave its name to the pack. This shows how hard working and persistent fell hounds could be. They were probably a little slower than modern fell hounds, as long hunts were far more common before the Second World War, but still they were incredibly useful and could account for several foxes during an average season. This was good news in mountainous and hilly country where foxes often preyed on farm livestock.

Foxes were possibly fleeter of foot back then too. For one thing they were far less common in those days, as much of the fells were heavily keepered and extensive fox control was carried out in many places. Also, far more people kept terriers and these would hunt and dig out foxes for farmers even when the hunt wasn't in that area. With fewer foxes, territories would be wider ranging and so Reynard could take hounds all over the place. Nowadays foxes are far more numerous with close inbreeding occurring and with territories consequently much smaller. That is why hunts, generally speaking, are not as long in more modern times (up until the ban, which came into force in England and Wales in 2005). Closely inbred foxes are not as strong as their ancestors were, and in past generations they would travel miles to find food, or a mate. More recently town and city foxes are dumped in the countryside and these poor urban specimens gave hounds very short runs indeed. Having said that, there were still a few modern foxes that could give hounds a long and good run, many of them dog foxes searching out a mate. These can range far and wide and, when disturbed, go 'straight-necked' back to home ground, giving exhausting runs in the process.

The first snows of 1926 arrived on **November 2nd** and Willie took his pack onto Carling Knott where they quickly had a fox afoot from the rocky heights of Black Crag. The snow showers made the going incredibly difficult as hounds pursued their quarry, which they finally lost at Friar Ghyll after much persistent work. The bad weather was setting in and served to emphasise the need to breed terriers that could stand up to the elements.

On **November 27th** Willie took his hounds and climbed right out onto the tops of the fells above Crummock Water and they eventually hit off a drag at Wandope (pronounced 'Wandup'), following the line with much difficulty all the way across the tops onto Grasmoor and to the incredibly rough landscape of Dove Crags. Here they marked with great enthusiasm: scratching at the unyielding rock and baying eagerly, frustrated at their inability to reach the skulking fox and calling for the terriers to come and shift it for them. Willie could hear them baying into the deep cavern as he crossed the fell tops and the terriers pulled harder at their couplings, answering the call of hounds, knowing Reynard was in and that at last their chance had come. This was a big cavern and no doubt Willie loosed a brace of earth dogs, which raced into the dark tunnel, each hoping to be first to their quarry. Reynard refused to bolt, as was often the case when they found themselves in a deep and pretty secure earth, so digging commenced and Willie could hear that the terriers were pressing their fox below.

The digging was hard, to say the least, but the fells in those days were inhabited by many quarrymen and miners and they knew how best to progress through difficult rock spots such as this one. They also knew how to do so safely, or as safely as possible, and so they eventually uncovered the two terriers who had already finished their fox below. It was an old grey dog fox and Willie was glad to account for it, as this type often turns to lamb-worrying during springtime.

December 2nd saw two foxes marked to ground in an earth at Low Fell End and both were bolted by the terriers and caught after short hunts.

On **December 4th** the hounds were drawing on Carling Knott again and a fox was eventually found lying up at Broken Ghyll. Hounds had been feathering at Broken Ghyll, their sterns held high, waving to and fro with more urgency as the scent gradually improved, making their way over the rocks and through the deep heather slowly but steadily. At first Reynard sat tight, but his nerve finally gave out and he was up and now fleet of foot, not looking behind him as he fled from the pack. Followers saw him as he climbed out of the ghyll and made for open fell and they cheered on their hounds, spurring them on to greater efforts. Their quest along a stale and cold drag suddenly swelled from whimpers to a full chorus of music which filled the morning air and stirred souls as no other

Willie Irving (junior) as a young man.

music could. Willie stepped up his pace in response and prepared for what he hoped would be a long and successful hunt.

Hounds fairly flew on the line as they made out for Black Crags, giving their Huntsman and followers a cracking view of some grand hunting, the swell of music being carried on the wind across the bleak tops where it could be heard, rising and falling, for miles around, even down in the villages as they came over the crest of the fell edge and made for the exposed mountainside. The fox made across open ground after lingering at the crags for a while and eventually crossed Whiteoak Beck, swollen after the autumn rains and now raging, tumbling and rumbling its way down into the valley beyond. Reynard took care crossing here, as did the hounds a few minutes later, because a careless bound would have meant one of them being swept away and drowned. The followers took care too, as did Irving, making certain his 'laal' terriers got across safely. In the past, several have been known to be swept away in Lakeland becks full to bursting with rain water, never to be seen again.

Their pilot now made for Melbreak Fell, passing Raven Crag and then dropping down into the low country, where he made for Lanthwaite. Hounds kept on coming as the scent held very well, the music swelling with each better line that came along. At times they slowed, lowering their voices, even falling silent on occasion, but then suddenly a lead hound would speak and the rest would be there, rushing forward to the line again and speaking and screaming for all they were worth. Then they surged ahead, trying to make up the ground they had lost at every check and pause.

The fox made out for Whiteside, but soon came off the fell again and crossed the vale. He now climbed Low Fell and made for Fellbarrow, where he steadily worked his way around the mountain in an attempt to throw the hounds off, but he couldn't shake them and so set his mask for the low country once more. This had been a long, hard hunt and Reynard had tried every trick in the book, sometimes managing to confuse hounds for a while, but four young hounds stuck to his line and they claimed his brush at last at Oak Bank Meadow. Hounds, followers and Huntsman alike were exhausted after such a long and arduous hunt, but it had all been worth it. Irving's pack, many of them young hounds, were now really working well as a unit and he was getting good results during this, his very first season.

December 16th proved a good scenting day and hounds followed a drag for quite some time from Rake Wood and eventually to Singleton Ghyll, where their fox was at last roused. They had a fast and furious hunt to Low Field and the pace was just a little too strong for Reynard, so he holed in a drain, hoping to shake off his pursuers. However, Willie had his small team of shackled terriers there and they soon bolted the quarry. It ran by Higham and then to Close Breast, where it again went to ground in a big underground chamber.

A terrier was put in and they were forced to dig. Reynard had himself a good vantage and it was difficult for the terriers to get to him, but in the end Ragman, one of the hounds, rushed in and drew out the fox, which was then worried by the pack. It had been a good hunt on a good scenting day, which was capped by a successful ending.

December 29th was a very memorable day and one that saw the pack split for almost the whole time they were out hunting. Hounds had two foxes afoot on Whinlatter and they split immediately, with the first lot making out for Hobcarton and then Grisedale Pikes, climbing out onto the high tops where it was cold enough to kill any man who lost his way and was stranded there overnight, or who had lost his footing, and injured himself. They then turned across the highest of the tops and ended up down at Lorton after a very fast hunt.

John Tyson Irving (known as 'Tyson'), Willie's older brother.

They checked badly here, but cast themselves, as fell hounds must do, and soon got going again at Shatton – down in the lowland pastures and woodland which are some of the best grazing lands in England. They headed to the railway and then back to higher ground at High Side, making for Ling Fell. From here the fox took them around this mountain for quite some time, but scent was good and he just couldn't shake them off. He had tried running through sheep, on railway lines, roads, wall tops, scree, bields (borrans), through becks and lowland streams, every obstacle he could think of in fact, but still they came, their haunting cry calling out for his brush, echoing and reverberating from the craggy fellsides all around. They claimed him in the end, after a long and difficult hunt that ended at Peter House, Bassenthwaite.

Meanwhile the other half of the pack took their fox round Wythop and back to Whinlatter, then by Sanderson Ghyll and away over the tops, next being seen at Whiteside Breast, where they bowled over and killed a fine dog fox after a run that had taken them across some of the highest and wildest spots in the district. Willie doesn't record whether or not terriers were used at all that day, but it is highly likely during such long hunts.

In those days there were not really any strict rules about terrier work and anyone within the vicinity of hounds, if they had a useful terrier with them of course, would put their dog to ground and hopefully this would usually bolt the fox. If the Huntsman or Whipper-in were hard on their heels, then the followers would hold back and await instructions, as hunt staff usually had the last say regarding this part of the hunting day. But if it was going to take the hunt staff some time to get there, then the nearest terrier would simply be used and Willie may not have known about it until a day or so later, if he heard at all. As a result, all of the terrier work could not possibly have been recorded. It seems that Willie only wrote up the memorable days, with more emphasis on the records of hound work, rather than terrier work. Having said this, it seems he still recorded much more terrier work than any other fell pack Huntsman, which tells us how passionate he was about his earth dogs, as well as his hounds.

January 8th was a red letter day for two reasons. They drew Carling Knott and soon had a fox on the go, enjoying a very fast hunt to High Nook and on to Melbreak Fell. Hounds pushed the fox hard and it was eventually forced to try for lower ground, descending the head of Melbreak and going past the kennels before making for Crummock Water, where they at last caught their fox in the lake itself. Scent was just too good and Willie's pack was now working too well for Reynard to shake them off. It is a thrilling sight for any Huntsman to see hounds take their fox past hunt kennels and it also tells him how good his pack are working when their quarry has to head for open water. For some reason hard-pressed foxes, particularly in the fell country, head for water and it is often their undoing, though some do succeed in escaping using this method.

February 8th saw one of the hounds, Croasdale, become fast in a borran (rocky earth) after the pack had run a fox to ground. They had followed quite a long drag to Wall Head Brow, where they unkennelled their fox, hunting it to Scaw where it 'holed'. It was too late in the day to do much about it, so Willie returned early the next day and, with the help of C. Smithson, T. Swinburn, F. Birkett and Tyson Stevenson, succeeded in digging out and releasing the hound from what would certainly have become its grave. Hounds will often get into a borran if they get the opportunity and they can easily become trapped. It is a tragedy when a hound is never seen again and one can only guess that it either fell from a crag or became trapped inside a rock earth.

February 15th saw the Melbreak pack have a good hunt that resulted in their fox going to ground at Millstone Moor Wood. However, hounds were driven away by followers of the now-defunct West Cumbria Hounds who had met at Threaplandgill that same day. I can imagine Willie was not impressed and no doubt sent these followers packing, for he tried the hole and his terriers worried the fox underground. Disputes are rare between foot packs in the fells, but when it does occur one can feel the tension involved in this 'clash' of packs, reading Irving's report. It seems the West Cumbria Hounds were hoping to bolt the fox for their own hounds to hunt, but Willie was having none of it and he accounted for his quarry despite this bit of an upset.

February 17th was one of the best of hunting days that season, despite a rather unpromising beginning. Willie drew for a fox for at least three hours before finally finding at noon by Silver Ghyll. A fast hunt followed and their pilot forced them to cross the river Derwent and on to Dunthwaite. The fox then took them round Nut Hill Wood and eventually re-crossed the river, going round Higham and on to Dunthwaite Breast where it finally went to ground. Willie's terrier, Riff, one he had brought with him from the Eskdale and Ennerdale Foxhounds bred down from his first pair of terriers, was entered and the terrier latched onto and drew out his fox from the earth. This is no mean feat and tells us something of the abilities of certain early Lakeland terriers. Willie set Reynard on his feet again, but he was caught after a short run.

Another was found in a hole at Kirkhouse Breast and again Willie entered his terriers, who accounted for their quarry below ground, before the dead fox was dug out and pulled clear of the earth. A dog and vixen were accounted for that day and Willie notes, in rather understated terms, that it was a "good hunting day".

LEFT: *Ennerdale schoolchildren, including the Irvings.*
RIGHT: *Ennerdale school today.*

February 22nd, a fast hunt was enjoyed from Whiteside and on to Dodd, which is the mountain above the present site of the kennels at Millar Place. The fox, being hard-pressed, then 'binked' at Quarry Crag and the terrier, Boss, was sent to shift it. Boss negotiated the narrow ledges with care and then bravely drove out the skulking 'Tod' from its rock shelf, which then gave hounds another fast run before eventually going to ground. However, the drama hadn't yet ended back at the crag, because Boss, after driving out the fox with such courage, fell down the crag and was injured. Even then the drama wasn't over. W. Gibson, a noted breeder of Lakeland terriers, put his own dog Crab into the earth where our fox had run in the hope of bolting it and Crab worried it underground while the digging operations continued. It seems Willie had remained at the crag in order to see to his injured terrier, Boss, while Gibson and a few others had followed hounds to where their quarry had gone in. Crab was a very good worker and saw off his fox, but in the process of being dug out a rock fell in on him and he too was badly lamed. Crab was undoubtedly one of the more important terriers of the pedigree Lakeland strains, but Willie doesn't go on to record whether or not Crab had to be put down because of his injuries. One can only hope that he recovered.

Foxes often calmly seek refuge (bink) on crag ledges either to watch the hunt from a safe vantage point, or when hard-pressed, and terriers were sometimes then used to shift them from such locations, though, of course, some crags were deemed too dangerous to allow terrier, or hound for that matter, access. So some foxes made good their escape using this method of getting out of reach of hounds. I believe the 'binking' of foxes on the crags had a bearing on the breeding of the Lakeland terrier, from around the 1870s. The Lakeland Terrier Association standard required terriers to be narrow at the shoulders and straight in the leg, both qualities which would be useful on a narrow shelf or ledge.

Narrow shoulders helped a terrier progress underground, obviously, but straight legs were not so necessary here, as bent-legged earth dogs had also proven useful, even in the fell country. However, when negotiating a narrow ledge at a steep and dangerous crag it is easy to see how narrow shoulders and straight legs would put the terrier in good stead, giving them easier access and making them more sure-footed. A broad-shouldered, bent-legged terrier would surely struggle, and be in more danger of falling, when negotiating such narrow ledges. Willie Irving, as well as other fell pack Huntsmen, often had foxes 'bink' and, though sometimes hounds could shift them, or perhaps stones thrown by followers would compel them to move, it usually fell to a stout-hearted terrier to do the job. True, earth work was the main employ of Lakeland terriers, or any other breed that worked with a fell pack, but an important part of their labour consisted of crag work and flushing foxes from dense coverts where hounds can't penetrate.

On March 8th a superb hunt was enjoyed, with hounds having their fox away after a find on Aiken Spars. It was a very misty day, but scent was good and they kept in touch as hounds made out for the high tops. Some of the followers had earlier climbed out onto the fell tops, acting as look-outs. The pack crossed by Hobcarton and Swinside, then on to Dodd Breast where Reynard sought sanctuary inside a rock earth. However, terrier breeder Thomas Rawling was there and he put in his terrier Gillert, one of the ancestors of most modern Lakeland terriers, pedigree and unregistered strains alike, which engaged its foe and was dug out after some time. Ernie Towers of Grasmere was also present and he helped dig out the fox whilst Willie undoubtedly drew for another. Gillert accounted for a fine vixen fox on that misty March day. This terrier had plenty of experience at fox, and no doubt other large quarry, as he also served at the Eskdale and Ennerdale pack. Gillert was one of the early terriers that produced the famous Kinniside strain of Lakeland bred by Bob Gibbons of Portinscale, as well as being one of the ancestors of Johnny Richardson's famous strain which are still found at the Blencathra kennels today.

On **April 5**[th] Willie drew out to near the top of High Crag and there hounds marked (tried digging at the hole) at Broken Rock Borran, a fearsome place that well illustrates how difficult fox control could be in this part of the world. Irving's Floss and Studholme's Squib were put in, but Reynard wasn't for bolting and so digging operations commenced, with the going more than difficult. Floss and Squib eventually worried their fox, but not before both had been badly bitten in the forelegs, which suggests their quarry got itself onto a ledge, from where it could do much damage as the terriers jumped at it in order to dislodge it. They succeeded in the end and another vixen was accounted for.

They were in the low country on **April 19th** and had enjoyed a hunt social the evening before at the village of Dean. Hounds found at Lucetta and holed their fox soon after, with J. Moore and W. Gibson putting their terriers to ground, no doubt as Willie's were rather few in number by this time. He had enjoyed plenty of terrier work in the last few weeks and no doubt had quite a few out of action. Vic, another famous terrier and one which Irving brought into his own strain, and a terrier named Jack, were entered and soon engaged their quarry, killing it below. The terrier-men dug it out and Irving notes that both of these terriers were young at this time, having been newly entered, so they were obviously progressing very nicely indeed. The vixen had mange and was the only fox suffering such a condition that they had seen all season.

Last day that season for the Melbreak Foxhounds was on **May 19th** and, though hounds hit off a drag for a while, they never got a fox going. But lambing troubles were coming to an end, so it didn't really matter. They had killed 53 adult foxes, as well as accounting for a few litters of cubs during lamb-worrying call-outs. They had had many good hunts and only a few blank days. Their young hounds had entered well, with two, Crafty and Lively, among the best in the pack. Trusty and Remedy were put down, as they were found to be useless, and young Ruby had to be put down that spring because she worried a lamb. Croasdale, the hound who was rescued out of a borran, also had to be put down because Willie stated, she was "in a bad way, wrong inside." One puppy, born in June 1927 out of old Comely from the Blencathra (bred by Jim Dalton) died of distemper, but the illness doesn't seem to have spread. Altogether there were twelve puppies bred that summer and the surviving eleven went out at walk all over the Melbreak country. Willie Irving had made rather a successful start to his career, aided by Tyson Stevenson as Whipper-in, and his hounds and terriers were proving to be among the best in the fells. He was also proving very popular with followers and farmers alike, and even in his first year, the hunt was becoming more financially and socially secure than it had ever been before.

An early photo of Willie and his Melbreak Pack.

CHAPTER 2

The Melbreak Hunt country

The Melbreak Foxhounds' country of Willie's youth was far bigger than it is today and it contains perhaps the greatest variety of landscapes in the whole of the county. There are huge mountains full of massive rocky outcrops and crags and deep-cut valleys lined with green fields, split by meandering rivers, becks and lakes. There are rolling hills lined with hedges and stone walls and carpeted with lush green pastures where pedigree herds of cattle graze, some to provide rich and creamy milk, cheese and yoghurt, others being fattened for some of the most tender of beef steaks. There are flat lands too in places, as well as a rocky coastline along the western side of the county, some of which makes up part of the Solway. There are also woodlands, big and small, and commercial forestry, along with some gentler fell or moorland country that is a little easier to traverse when following hounds. It is truly a hunt country of much variety and one that must have been a delight in Irving's day when busy roads were non-existent and trains were much slower, posing far less of a threat to hounds hunting their quarry.

Willie enjoyed the golden age of the Melbreak Foxhounds and his hunting was more-or-less uninterrupted by modern technology. Today busy roads, electric railways and the growing urban sprawl pose a major threat to any pack, even those in the fells. But those packs currently hunting trail scent within the law in England and Wales at least have the means to make certain that hounds are kept well away from road and rail. The Hunting Act may be repealed in time, or it may fall into obscurity through being impossible to implement, but even so, the biggest threat to hunting with hounds today remains the seemingly unstoppable tide of building roads, housing, industrial sites and shopping precincts.

The biggest danger to hounds in the fells in Irving's time were borrans and crags. Some hounds pushed themselves into borrans in an attempt to reach a fox run in by them. If the location wasn't known by hunt staff or followers, and the hounds had got away on their own and got into trouble, stuck in a borran, then there was a risk of them remaining there forever. Lost and trapped, sometimes a hound lost weight over several days and could then get out of a tight spot, but sometimes a hound could be trapped there and never discovered, one of the most heart-breaking sides to hunting in the Lakes. On occasion hounds got stuck on a crag ledge and then some stout-hearted person, usually Huntsman, Whip, or a keen and regular follower, would be lowered down on ropes and the 'cragfast' hound, or hounds, would be rescued. These hardy fell hounds could be stranded on a ledge in the open for a few days, enduring frost, or even snow, as well as icy rain and wind.

Borrans were a danger to terriers as well as hounds, and working out their fox from such places, and flushing foxes from crags made up quite a large part of the work of hunt terriers. But at least quarrymen and miners, skilled at working in rock, could be called upon to help out and advise when a terrier was trapped and many such tradesmen regularly followed the hounds.

The Melbreak country included the whole of the fells around Loweswater, Crummock Water and Buttermere and here is some of the highest, bleakest and roughest country to be found in the Lake District. Parts of the western side of Bassenthwaite were hunted, including the incredibly steep mountainsides above the lake. The northern flanks of Ennerdale Water were also hunted by the Melbreak, but most of the remaining Ennerdale country was hunted by the Eskdale and Ennerdale pack and, indeed, the Irving's lived just inside Dobson and Porter's country. Willie undoubtedly met Tommy Dobson when he was a young lad, but he was only twelve years old when Dobson died after catching a chill out hunting in 1910. It was common practise in the fells for hounds to visit village schools near the meet before heading onto the fells for a day's hunting and no doubt Willie enjoyed visits from the Eskdale and Ennerdale pack during his school years.

The Melbreak country ended just north of Cockermouth and

then stretched all the way to the Solway coastline, taking in ports such as Workington and Maryport. Here there are charming villages, rolling hills and patches of often-dense woodlands, which served as excellent coverts for foxes. The Melbreak often hunted the low country between the wars, but these days the roads are far too busy and the speed at which motorists travel makes it far too dangerous to have a pack of hounds loose in the wake of a fleeing fox, so much of it isn't hunted anymore. Few blank days were had in this part of the world, though several of the foxes made for the fells once disturbed. Many of Willie's hunts began in low-lying land, not far from the coast, but ended back on the fells where Reynard either escaped, or was accounted for.

1927/28 SEASON

Willie took up his duties again, gathering in his hounds from various local families, on **September 10th** 1927. But it wasn't until **September 17th** that they enjoyed their first hunt. They met at Carling Knott and had several foxes astir, no doubt a litter or two that hadn't yet dispersed, but scent was very bad and hounds just couldn't get on terms. Seven of the pack ran a fox to Scaw, but couldn't quite put enough pressure on it to secure a successful conclusion.

A wild misty morning spoiled a hunt on **September 19th** that ended with Reynard being lost after a good hunt on Melbreak, but **September 21st** proved a much better day. Hounds met at Whinlatter on a wet and misty morning and hounds were loosed into the large tracts of woodland. They found above Whinlatter Crags and a fast hunt ensued, with the music filling the woodland and fell country and guiding followers as they tried to keep up despite the grey screen of mist and light but persistent rain. Their fox took them down from the high country and eventually crept below ground on the lower slopes of Armaside Fell. It seems J. Norman was first at the scene and he put in his bitch, Red, the dam of Irving's Twist, which soon engaged its fox, while Norman dug to her. He quickly reached Red and drew out her quarry, which was set on its feet again, but soon accounted for by the hounds. Another fox was found shortly afterwards and Rival led the pack all the way until it holed (went to earth) at Lords Seat after yet another fast hunt that headed from the low country to the high fells – the reverse of the previous hunt. Damp, rather than sopping wet, conditions make for good scent, and this day proved no exception. No terriers were needed here, however, for the place wasn't exactly suited to provide security for a hunted fox and the hounds quickly got in among the rocks and pulled out their foe, killing it swiftly. However, another fox was found lurking in among the rocks and Willie's young terriers, just entering, got in and worried it. Hounds and terriers had accounted for three foxes: an old dog fox, a young dog fox and a young vixen, on a very damp and misty day. It was undoubtedly the loud cry of hounds that kept them in touch as a pack otherwise they would have struggled to account for even one.

October 1st saw hounds confined to kennels because of bad storms and floods, but **October 5th** proved a very successful day. Two foxes were roused from High Stile Breast after hounds had painstakingly worked out an overnight drag and the pack, as often happened, split in two. The first fox was run to ground at Brunt Bield, but the terriers couldn't quite get to it, so it was left after several attempts to shift it. However, the other hounds ran their fox in at High Stile and Alan Nelson's two young terriers succeeded in bolting it. Reynard was then bowled over after a short run.

The next hunting day was on **October 8th** at Whiteside. They found early on and ran out by Dodd and Swinside, on to Hope Ghyll and then back to Whiteside, where scent led them into the old quarry. Their fox had lingered awhile here and he was fresh put out again, though he didn't run for long. The cry of the oncoming pack resounded among the rocky outcrops and compelled him to seek shelter below. Willie put in his young terriers and they quickly found, latching onto their fox as it tried to bolt, which then dragged them out of the hole. Hounds were quickly in action and swiftly accounted for the fox, while the terriers were unharmed. These plucky little dogs can sometimes be killed by an over-excited pack rushing in on a fox that is being held by a terrier, though remarkably, fell hounds rarely make such a mistake. The day was warming up, scent was weakening, and so no more foxes were found.

October 29th was the day they met at Carling Knott again and scenting conditions were excellent. They found rather quickly and their pilot was away, making out across the fellside, through Holme Wood, High Nook and to Black Crag, with hounds soon picking up the line, their music swelling in unison. The deep bay of trusty Bellman could be heard, with Rival speaking to the line, the cry sounding above the others at times. And then Rally could be heard, as all quested for scent, surging ahead, then slowing and casting round. Marksman whimpered which was enough for the rest of the pack to rush to his side and cast all around, hitting the line and rushing forward again, but this time their voices swelled to full cry and from then on hardly a check hindered their progress.

With all the pack more-or-less together, hounds descended from Carling Knott and they were soon within the dense woodland at Holme, above Loweswater, their music more subdued here, but only because of the long lines of trees which soaked up much of the sound. Echoing softly around the wood and beyond, it reached the ears of followers and hunt servants who stood on the heights of the Knott and watched as hounds came out of the wood, their cry now more piercing, making across to High Nook and out onto the tops again. From here they made for Black Crag on a screaming scent.

Maud Irving, with her teddy bear and terrier Felix.

They slowed whenever they crossed scree, or went through bracken, but once they were on better ground the music rose to fever pitch and their pace quickened. Reynard then took them back by Bar Yeat and Godferhead and now on to Red How wood, where again the voices of hounds rattled around the dense woodland.

Laddie could be heard now, alongside Rival and Miller, Marksman and Rally. The crafty fox tried to stay ahead of the hounds by running them round woodland, but they just kept on coming and pressing him until, in the end, he left covert and was finally pulled down by Marksman and Laddie at Latterhead. It had been a wonderful hunt and Irving must have been overjoyed at seeing his young pack working so well together. However, the day hadn't yet finished.

Willie decided to make for kennels, but Rally hadn't had enough just yet and so was off, finding a fox and bringing it by Low Fell. Willie immediately loosed his pack and they quickly joined in, with a good hunt resulting that took them up Mosedale and on to Starling Dodd near Ennerdale. Here the fox went to ground. It seems the followers must have gone home, as Willie records he was on his own at the spot where the fox ran to ground. He put in Vic, the terrier walked by Jack Moore, and she was soon at her fox, which wouldn't bolt. Vic worried it underground, but she had to be left in as the body of the dead, or a fallen stone, was preventing her from exiting the earth. She wasn't got out until Monday morning, after a hard dig.

Meanwhile, Willie Porter's Eskdale and Ennerdale pack hunted a fox into the Melbreak country and put it to ground near Cleaves Ghyll (marked as 'Clews' on the map). It is not customary to use terriers to ground in another hunt country, so, when Willie Porter arrived on the scene, he asked Willie Irving to put in one of his terriers, which he did. It was a bad place, but still, Irving's terrier accounted for the fox in fine style.

Exactly which terrier Willie used is impossible to say, but my money would be on Riff, or Floss. Willie remarks in his diary that he "saw a good hunt" by Porter's hounds, before they ran their fox in. What a most successful day this had been and it was a fine demonstration of how effective a fell pack could be at controlling fox numbers.

November 1ˢᵗ, 3ʳᵈ and 5ᵗʰ saw hunting ruined, or called off altogether, because of gales, storms and floods and Willie states that it was "one of the roughest weeks ever known." On **November 12ᵗʰ** hounds enjoyed a hard three-hour hunt in difficult conditions, with a hard frost and poor scent to contend with. They found in Wilson Planting and finally killed a fine dog fox at Gillbrea, despite the hardships.

On **November 14ᵗʰ** Bellman was badly lamed in his left forepaw, the injury so severe that a Mr Hodgson, probably the local vet, had to reset it the next day. They were once again in the low country on **November 16ᵗʰ** and hounds met at Deanscales. The pack found a fox at Lucetta and ran it to ground at Cundard after a short run. Old Riff, one of Irving's early terriers from his time at Eskdale, was put in, but Reynard refused to bolt and so Riff worried it underground. They tried High Dyke Wood after their first fox had been accounted for, but a lot of deer were afoot and they spoiled the scent. Irving blew the gather on his horn and finished for that day.

November 23ʳᵈ proved to be one of the best and most memorable of any of Irving's hunts. Hounds found an old white-tailed fox at Williamson's Park and they had a fast hunt by Tutehill and Gilgarran, their pilot taking them through pasture and dense woodland, but scent was good and hounds owned the line well. Miller and Marksman, Rally and Rival, all took turns at leading and, at any checks, all cast independently, then came together again with wild excitement whenever scent was once again found, the eager lead hound whimpering and speaking, calling for the others to join in the chase as they sped on, rushing forward with the force of an oncoming tide. Reynard took them into woodland at Gilgarran and followers could hear the cry of their pack as they pushed on through the trees that were now almost bare after recent gales had stripped them of their colourful leaves. Over twenty hounds came out of the wood almost as one unit and then followed the line across the fields to Wythemoor Pit Wood where they discovered Charlie had gone to ground.

The hounds milled about the earth, the leaders with their heads and shoulders in, baying and digging, calling for blood as they tried to reach their quarry.

Willie wasn't too far behind with the terriers. He doesn't state which he used on this occasion, but it bolted the fox soon after entering its lair. This old fox had been hunted on several past outings and he was proving as cunning and as fleet of foot as before. He now gave hounds a long twisting hunt across the rolling hills and fields of the low country, heading north and taking them by Clifton Moor and Stainburn, going all the way to the river Derwent and up to William Pit near Clifton, where he hid on the bank. Not for long though, as the unshakeable hounds were soon on the scene and so he was away again, eventually making through the houses of Clifton and down the street, where he took refuge in the outside loo at Palmer's farm. Scores of people had joined the hunt by this time and they watched as Miller flushed the fox from the loo(!) and the rest of the pack then caught, and finally accounted for, this old white-tailed rival. The hounds had been hunting for just about four hours and they had covered possibly as many as twenty miles. Willie states that this was "the best we have had in that district with an old fox which had been run many times." During that hunt, as the hounds had come over Clifton Moor, they had upset a pony that was leading a cart full of coals, spilling its load as they raced past on the line of their fox. The old woman leading the spooked pony was heard to shout "who let aw them dogs owt?" as they raced past in full cry. It is hoped that Willie later made his peace with her.

The terriers had another busy day on **December 7th**, bolting a fox that had holed at Brunt Bield and then going on to flush it twice after it 'binked' at crags whilst the hunt progressed. They eventually accounted for this game fox.

They had a good hunt from Elva Plain on **December 17th** and to the river Derwent, hunting along the riverside until they almost reached Cockermouth town centre. Their quarry then took them by Cockermouth Gardens and the Drill Hall and then on through

Annfield, making out over the golf course and finally marking to ground at Dunthwaite. Reynard had taken them full circle before finally taking shelter underground. Two terriers were put in and they quickly worried their fox, but only one emerged afterwards. Squib was still to ground and had to be left in for two nights, finally being dug out after some very hard graft on the Sunday morning. Hunts took place on Fridays in those days, with few Saturday meets, so digging had gone on throughout Saturday and into Sunday morning. It was obviously a very deep and difficult earth, but eventually Squib was unearthed along with a sow badger she had turned her attention to after killing the holed fox. Prominent Melbreak follower John Roberts, who was present at that particular hunt, reported that Squib came out of there "hawf deed."

Much of the latter part of December saw hard frost settling in and so a few days were lost as it was deemed unsafe to loose hounds. A foot and mouth outbreak saw hounds confined briefly to kennels during early January. Willie then records that Jonathan Banks, the old Huntsman of the Melbreak, died on Monday January 9th and was

Melbreak supporters Hamilton Docherty (left) and Glaister.

buried on the 12th of that month, during a terrible storm. "One of the wildest days this winter", noted Willie.

During a week of hunting at Cockermouth starting **January 23rd**, hounds hunted several foxes, but caught few, with one crossing the river Derwent five times during one stint. And on the Friday, hounds joined the Blencathra pack after crossing the river and they finished on Binsey Fell – scene of many a hunt by John Peel and his hounds and one of his favourite locations.

On **February 1st** hounds marked at a difficult earth at Sawmill Ghyll. Reynard wouldn't bolt and so they were forced to begin what turned out to be a long and difficult dig and terrier and fox were finally reached at 6.15pm. It was a tragic end to a long day of toil, however, for the terrier Old Riff had been smothered by a fox that had clamped its jaws over his nose and mouth and thus preventing him from breathing.

This is an incredibly rare occurrence, but has been known to happen on a few occasions in the fells. The hunt was effectively over. Lakeland terrier breeder J. Bruce, having dug out the lifeless fox, carried it out of the wood and threw it over the fence, but it had been playing dead and suddenly sprung to life and ran off in the moonlight. Hounds had been coupled by this time, but they were loosed and a moonlight hunt ensued, with hounds finally catching a fine eighteen-pound dog fox at Wash Dub Wood after a fifteen minute run.

February 27th saw hounds at Gatesgarth for the week and on the Tuesday Bellman became trapped on a crag, but they rescued him safely. On the Friday hounds were hunting a fox and they soon joined by chance with the Eskdale and Ennerdale pack, with a long and fast hunt eventually taking them down into Eskdale after a fresh fox had been roused on Scawfell.

Willie was forced to stay the night at Eskdale, with some hounds still out, which he gathered on the way home the next day. One of his young hounds, Merry, however, never turned up and one can only guess at his fate.

March 7th was a good day and hounds had already killed a fox, before rousing another near Jonathan Planting. A very fast hunt involved hounds crossing the river Derwent and on to Blindcrake and Isel Big Wood. They then re-crossed and marked to ground at Andrew Bank. Willie put in his Tess and Scalehill Riff, but Charlie refused to bolt. He was worried by the brace of earth dogs and was dug out. They had finished a fine eighteen-pound dog fox – no mean feat for even a pair of working terriers. The kennel name of one of them, Tess, was Venus and she was an important bitch in pedigree bloodlines.

April 20th saw hounds loosed around lambing fields where a fox had been reported worrying sheep at Kirkgate Farm. Hounds found on Melbreak after a drag had been followed and an eight-hour marathon ensued in which they went by Hencombe, Low Fell, Mosser, Sossgill, Lamplugh Green, Blake Fell, Fell Dyke, then over into Ennerdale by Croasdale and Bowness Knott. Their fox now took them into Tarn Crag and then back by Blake and on to Lamplugh Green yet again, where, frustratingly, scent gave out after a long and hard day-long hunt. This was certainly a game fox and Willie was rather disappointed not to have caught him.

However, he was back at Kirkgate Farm on **April 25**th, with yet more lambs having been taken. They took up a drag and had it away from Pillar Rake, by Mosedale, High Cross, Bramley and Sossgill. Over Mockerkin Fell they ran and down to Lamplugh Green once more. Reynard then took them back to the high country at Carling Knott and was here put up afresh, finally making to ground at Burnbank, with hounds right behind him. A terrier was in as soon as Willie caught up and the fox was drawn, possibly by an earth dog, or maybe Willie had dug in, and was set on its feet again. However, he was rolled over and was the same fine dog fox they had hunted for eight hours only five days ago. Lamb-worrying ended at the farm so he was obviously the culprit. Huntsmen do not usually want such a fox bolting, so setting him back on his feet was an unusual move, but this was such a 'game 'un' that Willie no doubt wanted to give it the dignity of a chase before killing it.

The last hunt of the season was on **May 4ᵗʰ** from Rannerdale Knott, but the day was far too dry for good scent and they lost their fox after a while. Lamb-worrying ended early that season and they finished with forty-one foxes having been accounted for, with a few cubs also taken during lambing calls.

This was, by the standards of the times, not a massive total of foxes killed, but Willie did lose quite a number of hunting days due mainly to hard frost, severe gales and storms, with a few floods keeping hounds in kennel. Foot and mouth restrictions, though brief, also lost them a day or two. Tommy Swinburn had Whipped-in this season, because Tyson Stevenson had returned to farming.

The Melbreak country was, in many ways, easier to hunt than that covered by other fell packs, simply because of all the low country they covered. Having said that, there were also some fearsome spots and Honister Crag was probably the worst and most dangerous of them all. This place was quarried for top quality slate and stone and gave much employment to local people. Honister is incredibly steep and dangerous and men worked on the side of the crag, quarrying into the sheer rock face, like vast numbers of ants working into a large mound on the African Plain.

Quarrying made up a large part of the local employment in those days, but it was farming that was always at the heart of Lake District life: sheep farming among the fells, but also beef cattle and dairy herds, as well as chickens and geese. Pigs were often kept in those days and Cumberland ham was, and still is, a fine delicacy. Pigs were usually kept for home consumption and pig-killing time brought benefits to the whole community, because much of the surplus meat changed hands, either being swapped for other goods, or given away in the knowledge that, when other farming families killed their pigs, then they would find the favour returned.

Crops were also grown, especially corn and wheat, and meadows cultivated and harvested for winter feed, with barns full to bursting with fresh hay once the cutting, drying and gathering in had been accomplished. Whole communities came together at these times and helped each other, with large groups of children also sharing in the workload. One can easily imagine young Willie Irving, along with his siblings, relatives and friends, helping out in the Ennerdale district during his youth whenever major farming jobs needed to be tackled. Harvest could be a joyful occasion when spent in glorious sunshine, but sometimes farmers had to battle against the elements in order to gather in their crops and hay. Timing was critical but most of the dales were made up of related families in those days, far more so than now, so there were always helping hands to call upon and heavy workloads were made easier as all shared and helped each other out. Willie, along with friends and family, would spend much of the harvest time with terriers, collies and cur-dogs killing the large numbers of rats that spilled out of the gathered crops whenever they were being moved. These times no doubt helped instil in the young Willie that love of game terriers that lasted a lifetime.

Mining was the other important occupation locally and iron ore, coal and lead, as well as copper, had been clawed out of the earth throughout the Lake District for centuries. Today several old shafts are marked on ordnance survey maps, though many of the smaller pits are not marked. Even so, one can see how extensive mining was during the youth and middle years of Willie Irving. And disasters occurred at many of those pits. William Pit at Whitehaven (not to be confused with the one at Clifton) was the scene of a terrible disaster when an explosion caused death and injury on a large scale and was considered a national disaster.

Eddie Pool of the Ullswater Foxhounds, who hunted with Anthony Barker when he was Huntsman of that pack during the Second World War, tells tales of mining for lead in the Ullswater district and of how several folk died, not just in the mines themselves whenever they flooded, or when tunnel roofs fell in, but also because of small flecks of lead settling in the lungs of the miners, eventually making it impossible for them to breathe. His stories are horrific and Eddie had family members die of such conditions. His descriptions of them lying in their beds, unable to get about anymore, struggling for breath and waiting to die, are truly heart-rending. However, mainly iron ore and coal was mined in the Melbreak country; the coal was more prevalent towards the coast, and the iron ore mainly inland, the red-tinged water of the becks betraying a large iron content in many areas.

1928/29 SEASON

Willie took up his duties for his third season as Huntsman on **September 15th** and started with 26 hounds and 6 puppies. Fell packs in earlier times usually had fewer hounds than this, with most having only a dozen or so in kennel, so it says something of the prosperity of the Melbreak pack that they were able to keep as many as they did. They obviously enjoyed good support from followers, villagers and farmers throughout their country. Their first hunt was **September 18th** and they had a good hunt from Hope Ghyll, but lost their fox due to unfavourable scenting conditions, which is pretty typical of this time of year.

October 15th saw hounds enjoying a good hunt, notable because Squib, a terrier from the Coniston country and an ancestor of the modern pedigree Lakeland, became trapped at Pardshaw Crag. Willie doesn't state whether this was an earth, or whether Squib had flushed a fox that 'binked' on a ledge, but, nevertheless, she was stuck for some time before a rescue had been effected.

The opening meet was on **October 18th**. The previous early meetings were to train young hounds how to hunt foxes and to increase the fitness of the pack. Opening meets are the official start to the season and it was attended by lots of folk and they started at Carling Knott, but had to abandon it because of a 'terrible storm' that set in.

November 1st was a better day and hounds drew Rannerdale Knott and Whiteless Breast, where they had a fox up at last, after hounds had worked hard casting through deep heather and over rock and scree, which makes for incredibly difficult hunting country, but still, the hounds pressed their fox hard as it made for the high tops and eventually holed at Wandope Crag. Willie put in two of his terriers, Squib (who had obviously recovered from her ordeal two weeks earlier) and Felix, and they quickly found their quarry as it tried to dodge them among the rocks. Charlie wasn't keen on bolting, however, so was duly worried underground. They eventually dug out the brace of earth dogs after some hard graft, along with the carcass of a young dog fox.

Their next outing was **November 3rd** and they drew at Rogerscale, but didn't find until they got to Red How Wood. They then enjoyed a fast hunt with good scent conditions prevailing and it took them

Willie Irving (with hound jumping up) and his pack assemble in Cockermouth town centre.

down to Bottoms and by Whinfell. Hounds fairly flew on the line and familiar voices rang out into the cold autumn morning air, with Ragman and Royal, Miller and Marksman, Bellman and Cleaver, along with a host of other pack members, adding their thrilling tones to the swelling music and crossing the rough fell country at a rattling pace.

Willie and the followers did their utmost to keep up with them, but they could not resist the temptation to stop and view hounds at any vantage-point they could find. And what a thrilling sight greeted them as hounds pushed on, ever on, in the wake of their fast-fleeing fox. This was a good hill fox and Irving was forced to take every short cut possible in an attempt to keep his hounds in view.

Reynard now climbed out by Dodd, Watching Crag and then away by High Mosser and Beech Hill. Charlie came back by Low Fell End and crossed to Melbreak Fell where our fox 'binked' on the crags at Pillar Rake. The terriers weren't needed this time though, as Laddie negotiated the narrow ledge and flushed his fox from the crag, with the rest of the pack soon onto the line.

They viewed their fox down the fell now and finally caught it behind the fell wall close to the old kennels at the foot of Melbreak. It was an old vixen who had undoubtedly given hounds the slip on several occasions. What a superb hunt this had been and one that had taken hounds on a long and difficult run, which was at last rewarded after two-and-a-half hours.

November 27th was a memorable day, but not for good reason. The hounds had a fox away from Harrot (pronounced 'Harrod') Fell and they enjoyed a long hunt, but eventually ran out of scent at Embleton. In the meantime Samson, one of the hounds, had gone missing during this hunt and it was later discovered he had been killed by a motor car. Few automobiles were on the Lake District roads in those days, so the accident was all the more tragic.

The Melbreak pack met at Lamplugh Cross on **December 8**[th] and they soon had a couple of foxes on the move, but a hard frosty morning meant scent was poor and they eventually ran out. However, Dido,

Badger and Charmer got away on a fresh fox and eventually killed it at Ennerdale Water, on the lakeside just below Gillerthwaite.

On **February 9**th hounds put a fox off at Hobcarton after drawing up through Hope Gill, with a fast hunt following which took them by Long Crag, Eel Crag and Wandope. Charlie then took hounds through Bannerdale Side and back up Grasmoor Top. Out by Eel Crag they ran once again and then through Addacombe, over Wandope and away to Newlands Hause. Reynard finally holed in Robinson, possibly at the crag. Willie put in one of his game terriers, maybe Felix, or Squib, or possibly Vic, and Charlie bolted soon after, once the terrier had worked its way through the twisted and piled-up mass of rocks and had forced its quarry to make a bid for the open once more, with much barking, nipping and teasing, always looking for its chance to get in a fatal bite if Reynard loitered for too long.

On this occasion Charlie now made for Gatesgarth and then back on to the high fells by Littleton, High Snab and Birkrigg, going over Rowling End and then on to Barrow. Reynard, hard-pressed by the relentless pack of hounds in full cry, headed down to the lower country and made out across the Bottoms until he was finally pulled down at Ullock Farm, not far from Portinscale village.

This had been a hunt of vast distances when one considers the deep valleys and high fells covered by fox and hounds and had been a testing run indeed. The day hadn't ended just yet, though, as a few hounds got away on another fox and killed it at Force Crag. Two foxes hunted and two foxes accounted for. That is no small achievement when one looks at the map and discovers that this hunt led hounds, hunt staff and followers across some of the highest and bleakest country in England, covering many miles as hounds run.

The last fortnight in February was lost to severe frost and incredibly dry conditions, which resulted in no scent at all. Willie took hounds out on exercise and tried one or two places, but found no holding scent whatsoever. He had little good hunting in March either, because of yet more dry and frosty weather and only killed two foxes on lambing calls around the Buttermere district.

By the last hunting day on **May 25th**, only 29 foxes had been killed
that season. A lot of days had been lost to bad weather and dry conditions which made hunting nigh-on impossible at the back end of that
season. The terriers had had plenty of work worrying, bolting and
flushing foxes from crags, but still, it was a disappointing end to a
season that had seen some excellent early hunting.

*Captain Willie (second from right, front row) with his cup-winning Bootle
football team.*

CHAPTER 3

Guide Races and Association Football

The Irving family had moved back north to Bankhouse Farm when Willie was still an infant and, as we have seen, he went to school at Ennerdale Bridge. Much of his free time, when he wasn't working on family farms, following hounds, or hound trailing, was devoted to guide races in the summer and, in the winter, football. Guide races later became known as fell races, or fell running, and early reports from his contemporaries state that he was very hard to beat. He was competitive, strong and extremely fit and he won several of these races, or was at least in the top three. He was also a very good football player and one can imagine him developing a love of this sport whilst playing in the schoolyard during his morning and dinner breaks.

The family farmed mainly low country, whilst they undoubtedly had grazing rights on the fells, though much of it could not be said to be prime farmland. Sheep were often kept on the fells and brought down to the low country at lambing and shearing time, then returned to the high country for a while, with lambs later being brought back to the lowlands for fattening in readiness of sheep sales. It was undoubtedly a struggle and this may explain why William and Sarah had headed south for a time. Willie was outgoing, cheerful and lived a very active and full life and people loved him. He had a way with folk which enabled him to get on well with everybody, rich and poor alike, and it was no time at all before he was winning races and was being picked for the local football team.

Willie completed his schooling at Ennerdale and it seems that the family then moved to another farm at Bootle. Certainly by the age of eighteen, and possibly much earlier, Willie had started working full-time in the farming industry and it is very likely that he was working for Willie Porter at Eskdale. It is possible that he worked at

Willie (next to starter) about to take part in a fell race.

his parents' farm, but it is more likely that his brother Tyson Irving, the eldest lad, assisted his father around the family farm.

What we do know is that Willie obtained his first terriers in 1916 and that they were from the Eskdale and Ennerdale hunt country, which tells us of Willie's association with this hunt during those early years. Willie Porter lived at Field Head Farm, Eskdale, and combined the business of hunting hounds with his farming duties, though he undoubtedly needed much assistance to cope with a heavy workload.

It appears that, by 1916, Willie was working for the Eskdale and Ennerdale Foxhounds Huntsman and no doubt he also assisted on any hunting days he could attend. He was not an official Whipper-in though, until later in the 1920s when he was appointed not only to help around the farm, but also to Whip-in on hunting days. Willie would no doubt stay with the Porters, or in lodgings at Eskdale, for much of the week, returning home to Bootle whenever he could, until, probably in 1923, he moved in with the Porters permanently and became part-time farmer, part-time Whipper-in at the hunt. He served for three seasons as Whip to the Eskdale and Ennerdale pack and it seems he also became a serious terrier breeder during those early years. From 1916 Willie began to make his contribution to the Lake District working terrier scene, and what a massive contribution he would go on to make!

Willie Porter had a reputation second-to-none at that time as a top breeder of working terriers, mostly coloured fell types, though several he bred were also white, due to much fox terrier blood being used on fell strains during the latter half of the 1800s and this practise continued well into the twentieth century. Many were the white-bodied terriers that served at the Eskdale and Ennerdale pack during both the Porter and Dobson eras. Willie Irving learnt much from Porter, but also from others, as some of the best terrier breeders in the north hunted with this pack during those times, as well as with the Melbreak.

Along with his love of farming and hunting, Irving excelled at guide races and football and he was eventually appointed Vice-Captain of Bootle football team for the 1924/25 season, dividing his time between Eskdale and Bootle village. Bootle was in the Millom and District League at that time and it was during his Captainship that they triumphed in the District Cup. He was already a champion fell runner, but now he also became a champion footballer and much

Willie Irving and the Bootle football team which triumphed in the cup final.

of this was put down to his leadership skills.

He was truly proving to be a leader of men and had made quite a name for himself in the sporting arena in particular, though he also had much experience with both hounds and terriers. He saw an advert in the local paper in the early months of 1926 for the position of Huntsman to the Melbreak Foxhounds and, no doubt encouraged by Willie Porter who thought very highly of his Whipper-in, as did Mrs Porter who took good care of him at her home, he applied for the job. Many, in fact, applied for the job, but his application stood head and shoulders above the rest and was gladly accepted. Thus Willie Irving became the new Huntsman of the Melbreak Foxhounds – a pack with which he had already hunted on previous occasions. The chance to have as Huntsman a young man who excelled at sports, was very fit and already had much experience of hunting hounds and working terriers behind him, despite his young age, must have been irresistible to the Melbreak committee members.

Willie rounds the cairn on another fell top.

Fell runners before the off: Willie Irving is third from right.

1929/30 SEASON

Willie began work for his fourth season with the Melbreak on **September 14th** and they killed during their very first outing on **September 17th** at Thomson Planting, after drawing and hunting through Whinlatter.

September 30th was a day of bad scenting conditions, but Willie still managed to account for two foxes with the terriers from an earth at Dunthwaite, after meeting at Higham.

Hounds met below Rannerdale on **November 6th** and they drew the fells, eventually finding after quite a long time of casting at Dove Crags, high on Grasmoor. A long and difficult hunt followed and hounds persisted in sticking to what was often a painfully slow line. They crossed the fells and eventually went by Robinson and then back in by Barrow Fell. Details are a little scanty about this extraordinarily long hunt, but they eventually ran their pilot to ground at about 11pm! Willie doesn't explain clearly what happened, simply stating that the fox holed, but that it was worked out and killed. Either Willie dug his fox out using a terrier by the light of lanterns, which was customary in the fells when digging after dark, or he returned the next morning to account for it after having blocked it in overnight. Or, indeed, he may have meant that hounds managed to work it out and kill it after it had gone in, not an unknown occurrence in the fells, as some hastily chosen lairs prove to be really quite shallow.

November 16th witnessed hounds meeting in the low country at Deanscales, with much of the fell country having been covered in snow during previous days. The pack found a fox lurking at Lucetta, which seems to have been an almost sure find in those days. Another grand and long hunt followed, which saw Reynard eventually making for Low Fell and then onto the shores of Loweswater. He was hard-pushed by the oncoming pack and he just couldn't throw them off, no matter what trick he conjured along the way, so, having tried every other cunning rouse in the book, he decided to take to the lake to see if this worked. He swam Loweswater followed by the pack and then found himself back on dry ground, heading now for the higher fells at Burnbank and across to Lamplugh Fell. Hounds fairly flew, with Cleaver, Ragman, Royal, Marksman and others adding their voices to the haunting cry which kept followers in touch, with Laddie pushing for the lead, along with other superb hounds such as Bellman and Rival. Scent remained very good for most of the way, but as is often the case when a fox takes to swimming a lake, he didn't give off

A rare early photo of Willie (2nd left) with the Melbreak pack. The whipper-in is thought to be T. Swinburn.

quite as much scent afterwards and as he tired he gave off even less, which is why hounds finally lost their quarry at Teathes, near Ennerdale Bridge, after a rattling hunt that had been of long duration.

The Melbreak pack met at Kirkstile on **November 21ˢᵗ** and they drew the low country and then moved onto Carling Knott, where they had a fox away. In fact, there turned out to be two foxes on the move as hounds split soon after, one lot holing their foe at Goose Bield and the other lot being taken out onto the high tops in the direction of Ennerdale Water. Willie was soon up with his first lot of hounds and two terriers were put into Goose Bield in the hopes that Charlie would bolt. There are some strange place-names in the fell country and I believe this borran might have earned its title after a goose was taken from a lowland farm and was eaten by the fox at this location, which was later accounted for by the hardy fell-hunters of old. Which terriers were used is not recorded, but those who could have been out that day were Rex, Nip, Twist, Felix, Vic, and Squib. All were serving at the hunt at this time. Whichever went to ground in this rocky lair that day, they were game for certain, for they worried the fox below ground, after it had refused to bolt.

Willie now set off after the other hounds, no doubt leaving trusted followers at Goose Bield to dig out the terriers and their now-dead quarry, and he at last found the rest of the pack over towards Ennerdale, where they hunted their fox around the high fells and eventually ran Reynard in at Bowness Knott. Willie states that "it had to be left", but doesn't say why. This spot may have been just inside the Eskdale and Ennerdale country, or it may have been that the place was a known death-trap to terriers.

Hounds met again two days later at Dean on **November 23ʳᵈ**, at the village school, which helped keep youngsters in contact with a traditional part of Cumbrian life. Willie was popular with all he met, especially children, and proved a great ambassador, even during those early days, for the tradition of fell hunting. Hounds marked an earth at the inevitable Lucetta wood and the terriers again worried their fox below ground in typical fashion. Lakeland terriers of those days were fox killers in the main and many foxes were accounted for under-ground, though carcasses were usually dug out, even if it took a day or two to do so.

November 29ᵗʰ was a traditional Shepherd's Meet (*see page 128*) and hounds enjoyed a superb hunt, but failed to kill, with poor Ragman, one of Irving's best and most trusted hounds, falling from a ledge into Bull Ghyll, Honister, where he died as a result. The weather had turned and **December 21ˢᵗ** proved to be a bad day indeed and hounds, after meeting at the Wheatsheaf, Lorton, had a slow and difficult hunt to Grisedale Pike, but there was thick snow on the fells and it was very cold, especially on higher ground, so Willie blew 'the gather' after trying to get hounds going over at least three or four hours, with the elements getting the better of them in the end.

December 26ᵗʰ saw hounds drawing Whiteside after the Boxing Day meet and they at last had their quarry away from Gasgale Ghyll. They then had a long hunt by Hobcarton, Long Crags, back by Grisedale Pike and across to Swinside. They then went through Hope Ghyll and back onto Whiteside once more. To Whin Benn now they chased, where Reynard doubled back and came through Whiteside Breast, giving spectacular views to some of the followers as it made out for Dodd and finally crept to ground at Swinside. Willie put in one of his terriers and it soon found. It was a spectacular bolt, as the terrier had latched onto its prey and the big hill fox came out of the rocks with it hanging on. Reynard didn't get far though and hounds soon pulled him down after one of the best hunts of that season so far.

January 4ᵗʰ witnessed hounds drawing Grasmoor and they 'fanned out' with their noses questing around the heather and rock, their sterns held gaily, moving to and fro in keen anticipation of finding scent, however much or little there might be. Willie encouraged his pack with a few softly spoken words until, at last, a fox was seen sneaking away through deep heather just ahead of hounds. Willie's voice now rose as he cheered on his pack and they were quickly onto the scent, with all speaking and going away as their chorus rang through the valleys and echoed among the rocky outcrops and sheer-drop crags, chasing over the fell tops and dying away to far distant places. Scent proved very strong this day and the pack made good ground as they climbed Grasmoor and headed out onto the bleak, wild tops. The fox took them across the top of Dove Crags, shunning the relative safety of ledges and rockpiles found there, then across the top of Coledale and on over to Eel Crags. Charlie turned down Addacombe Top and over to Whiteless, Low Bank, then doubled back to Whiteless where he made for a rocky lair and reached it just before the hounds could claim his brush. Willie had managed to keep in touch very well indeed and he was more than happy to see most of his young hounds still with the pack when the hunt came to an abrupt end at this borran. Willie put in a brace of terriers and Reynard was worried underground after a fine and exciting hunt.

January 25th saw many hunting folk turn out for a meet at Peel Wyke and Willie drew all round Wythop Woods, Barf and almost to Thornthwaite, without even a whiff of scent. The day wore on and eventually he made back for the kennels, but, unfortunately, one of his most promising young hounds, Melody, picked up some poison on the way home, though he doesn't say whether or not she died as a result. I think it likely, however.

January 28th was a good day and hounds enjoyed a very good hunt by Dodd and on to Rogerscale, Mosser and Bramley, which is quite some distance as hounds run, after meeting at Oak Bank. Charlie turned back by Ask Hill and finally made to ground at Low Fell End, in one of the rocky bields there. Willie arrived some time later and put in Nip and Twist, which worried their fox among the rocks. Irving and some of the keener followers managed to dig out their quarry and it was a fine dog fox.

They were at Cockermouth on **March 14th** and found a fox in Higham Big Wood, with a fast hunt taking them all the way to Bothel Craggs where it may have holed, or possibly binked. It seems the hunt may have stopped for a while about here, but was soon got going again and

LEFT: *Willie with a Fell Race trophy.* RIGHT: *With fellow running mates.*

Charlie came back by Sunderland village and made for the original starting point of Higham Big Wood again, where he finally went to earth.

Willie found hounds marking when he arrived and Rex was loosed from the couplings. The terrier entered cautiously, sniffing the entrance that had been dug up somewhat by eager hounds intent on reaching into the earth and pulling out their fox, then he disappeared below. He pushed himself on through the narrow tunnels, continually testing the often-stale air for scent, twisting and turning and pausing for a few seconds whenever he came to a fork, with one passage going right, the other left. His experienced nose quickly told him which route to take and on he went, pushing himself along with his back legs, his forelegs digging into the earth and pulling himself forward.

And finally scent grew so strong that Rex knew his quarry was immediately ahead of him and he pinpointed its exact whereabouts, despite the pitch-blackness in which he had to work. Irving remained silent above, making certain too that all followers made no sound. The hounds were held back by Tommy Swinburn, who helped out with whipping-in at that time, and in the silence round the earth, Irving knew the very second Rex found, as the dog bayed and lunged at his quarry, quickly gripping it and finally getting in a fatal bite to the throat. When the plucky terrier was dug out a little later he had finished his foe and was still eagerly ragging the warm, but now lifeless, carcass. He had been bitten a few times himself and needed cleaning up, so Willie left one or two keen followers to backfill the earth, while he took hounds and terriers back to where they had stayed during hunting that week in the Cockermouth district. There he treated Rex's wounds, checked over his pack, then fed and bedded them down. And then it was off to the Embleton Hunt Ball that night where they had a cracking do. Willie states that it "was a big success."

March 18th saw hounds drawing Carling Knott and the surrounding district, but it snowed heavily and no fox was found. They lost a couple of days hunting that week simply because of the depth of snow. Snow can hide sheer drops between rocks, or can make edges of crags seem to extend much more than they actually do, so hunting in such conditions can be lethal to both hounds and followers. In heavy snow they often cancelled altogether, or went to the low country where conditions were usually much safer.

March 26th witnessed two foxes being put off in Higham Big Wood, with hounds splitting and going away on both. Mounted Huntsmen can often stop one group of hounds and bring them back to join the others, but a foot Huntsman can only watch as hounds split, sending the Whipper-in to follow one lot, whilst he follows the other group. One fox gave hounds a very good hunt round Ouse Bridge and on to Bassenthwaite Lake, where Charlie turned and made once again for Higham, where this hunt began. He carried on and made to earth at School Fell. It seems Willie wasn't far behind, for he put in his Terrier, Twist, who is yet another ancestor of modern pedigree Lakeland terriers, as well as many strains of unregistered Lakelands.

Twist was a very sound worker and single-handedly worried the fox below ground. Irving then went in search of the other pack and discovered that they had crossed the Derwent and had gone on to Binsey and Torpenhow. They then headed back by Bothel, Sunderland Village and this second fox was finally run into near Bothel Craggs after a superb and incredibly exciting four-hour hunt. What a day for the Melbreak! Two foxes put off almost at the first draw and both giving good hunts and finally being accounted for.

March 28th saw hounds out yet again, but Irving's diary isn't clear as to exactly which area they hunted, though it was possibly Dunthwaite. What it does tell us, however, is that hounds marked a fox to ground and in pursuit of it, Willie entered Studholme's Squib and J. Moore's Vic. Either this pair of terriers were on loan to the Melbreak for the season, or it is possible that Irving owned them himself but put them out at walk during the summer with followers Studholme and Moore. Either way, this brace of earth dogs, typey Lakeland terriers that made up part of the foundation stones for the pedigree strains, duly worried their fox below ground and digging commenced. Irving unearthed his terriers, along with an old vixen, sometime later.

April 18th was the traditional Good Friday meet and Willie drew blank for quite some time and distance until, at last, at Eel Crag they had a fox on the run, which gave them a good hunt to Gable Crag and beyond. They had a particularly exciting hunt around Yew Crags and Reynard was then hunted, Willie writes, "from one bink to another" and undoubtedly the terriers had a busy and hectic time of it, shifting the fox from its precarious lodgings. Charlie was finally accounted for by the persistent pack close to the Honister road. It was during this hunt that Willie was lamed whilst following in the wake of his pack and so, on **April 21st** Tommy Swinburn and 'Mowdie' Robinson (Mowdie is a name for a mole in Cumbria and Robinson was, among several other occupations, a mole catcher) took charge of hounds, but they failed to find that day.

Tommy and Mowdie took hounds again on **Tuesday April 22nd** after a very successful hunt function the night before, but, again, no foxes were found in the low country, not even at Lucetta.

Willie, having been laid up for only two days with a bad injury, took up his duties again on **April 25th**, though he wasn't fully recovered and he states that he was "a bit crocked." He loosed his gallant pack up Mosedale and they had a slow drag out to Scaw. They went by

Wall Head Brow, then back to Scaw, but struggled with a bad scent. However, they found an old vixen and three cubs lying in at Gale Fell Brow and Willie dug them out with a terrier. He accounted for the vixen, but managed to get the cubs out alive and he then took them back to kennels and fostered them onto his terrier bitch, Felix, who obviously had a litter of pups at the time. The vixen had been killing lambs, so Willie had no choice but to deal with her. What he eventually did with the cubs is unknown, but he may have sold them to help restock another hunt country after the native population had been decimated by disease, or suchlike. This was a custom of those times: to encourage foxes so long as they weren't lamb-killers.

A lambing call resulted in hounds running out of scent as the sun got up on **May 1st** and this springtime seems to have been pretty quiet after that, with no reported troubles, except for some pheasants being taken at Gilgarran. Willie went to deal with the guilty fox on **Thursday May 15th** and he found a dog fox skulking in a drain close to a slag bank near the railway, which he duly accounted for with the terriers. End of troubles!

It had been a hard, but good season with the hounds hunting very well indeed, with young terriers also entering well and proving very useful. Despite some days lost to bad weather and a few blank days because of keepers being a little over-keen with the gun at times, the Melbreak accounted for forty-seven foxes throughout that season, which was quite an accomplishment, when one considers the vast terrain hunted and the shortage of foxes in some areas.

Willie Irving loved Guide Races: a sport which had originated with mountain guides. Tourism in the Lake District had boomed following the Romantic poets Wordsworth and Coleridge in the early 1800s and this interest continued throughout the Victorian era. Guides were considered essential by the wealthy tourists in search of the very best of picturesque views, but many were daunted by

The Melbreak pack assembles at the Queen's Head, Cockermouth.

the mountainous landscape. The awe-inspiring terrain had, in fact, kept tourists at bay for many years, until more adventurous travellers began to write about the area and it was discovered that 'terrible monsters and fearsome beasts' didn't live in the remote valleys, or on the fell tops after all!

Mountain guides began racing each other up and down these mountains during lulls in employment and so the sport of fell running was born. By the 1920s this sport had reached heights of popularity and Willie won many races during this decade. It seems he had stopped racing by the end of the 1920s and took up training fell runners instead. Two of his best young hopefuls were Albert 'Fish' Thomas, who became his Whipper-in, and Billy Conkey. Billy was very successful indeed and went on to win at Grasmere Sports, which was the premier event for Guide Races. Both Albert and Billy were called up for the Second World War and they returned safely, but not to race anymore.

Billy Conkey was born at Irton, Eskdale on October 10th 1914 and ran his first competitive race at Bassenthwaite, with his first win being at the Eskdale show. His training consisted of three to five miles across rough country twice a week and this training was led by Willie Irving. It was in 1938 that he won at Grasmere, not long before he went to war. His Grasmere triumph was over an incredibly steep and difficult two mile course which led right to the fell top and back and he completed his win in 13 minutes and 48 seconds. He was a labourer who lived and worked at Lorton during the 1930s and he distinguished himself serving at Burma during the war.

Other noted fell runners of the time included John Roberts, who actually raced against Willie in his last-ever competitive run on the fells at Ireby Sports. This was Roberts' first race and Irving's last. The Garners of Embleton, Geordy Woolcock, Colin Johnson, Jack James, Jim Thorburn, Joe Grisedale, Ralph Gilpin (whom Willie greatly admired) and Ronnie Robinson were all top fell runners during the 1930s.

Billy Conkey, one of Willie Irving's protegés, winning the Fell race at Grasmere Sports.

Maud Irving, wife to Willie Irving (junior), at High Thrushbank in 1926.

CHAPTER 4

Married Life and new Kennels

Willie Irving took up farming as an occupation when he left school and it seems he spent much time in the Eskdale district, eventually being employed by Willie Porter of Field Head Farm, as we have seen. What is not known, however, is exactly when he took up his duties at the Porter farmstead. However, he certainly worked for this family during the mid 1920s during which time he also served at the Eskdale and Ennerdale pack as Whipper-in. He assisted with hunting and caring for hounds and terriers, as well as working on the farm itself, and whilst at Eskdale he met a Miss Maud Black of Boot, which lies in the upper reaches of the Eskdale valley.

The Black family were originally from Scotland and they settled in the Lake District during the 1700s. Their chosen settlement was at Sawrey in what is now known as 'Beatrix Potter country' and they made a living from burning wood, which they gathered from the woodlands of this area, to produce charcoal. It seems they were originally farmers, but it was some time before they managed to take a working farmstead at Wasdale Head Hall Farm. The family moved again some time later and arrived at Eskdale. Here they farmed at Ghyll Bank and Howes Farm. Many years later, Willie met his future bride there. He may have worked at her parents' farm, or maybe he met her through hunting connections. The pair fell in love and were married sometime during the mid 1920s.

Willie and Maud were certainly married by the time he became Huntsman of the Melbreak pack and the cottage that came with his newly acquired post was at High Thrushbank, near Loweswater. This is where Willie and Maud were living when they had their first child, also named Maud, on September 15th 1926, the very same day that witnessed Irving, as newly appointed Huntsman, account for a

fox with his terriers in a drain at Rogerscale. Pearl was the second
daughter and she was born nine years later on May 3rd 1935, after
her parents had moved from High Thrushbank. Willie was staying
at Buttermere in an attempt to catch up with lamb-worrying foxes
at the time of Pearl's birth, but he surely must have made for home
to see his new baby before returning from the Buttermere Valley on
May 6th where he had accounted for three adult foxes and quite a
number of cubs. Willie and his wife had much more than successful
fox control to celebrate and no doubt he 'wet' the baby's head on
more than one occasion!

The hunt kennels in those days were situated at the Banks' farm.
Jonathan Banks had been Huntsman of the Melbreak Foxhounds for
many years, before Richard Head took the helm, and hounds had
been kennelled at the Banks' family farm at the foot of Melbreak fell
for many, many years, inside a small outbuilding built onto the end of
a barn. It is, in fact, just possible that hounds had been kennelled here
from the very early days of the hunt, as Melbreak Fell is what gave the
pack its name in the first place, suggesting that hounds had originally
been sited there. It is also possible that farmers in the locality shared
the kennelling of a few hounds and they brought them together on
specified hunting days, or when livestock was being preyed upon.
This was certainly the custom with regard to the early farmers packs,
which is what the Melbreak was. The old kennel is still to be found
there to this day, nestling at the foot of Melbreak Fell, though the
open yard is gone, where hounds could sit out in the fresh air. The

*The wedding day of
William Irving and
Maud Black.*

kennel building itself has no windows and isn't very well situated, being on the north end of the barn and thus out of the sun for much of the day. The east side though, where the yard was, would get quite a bit of sun in the morning, and the kennel must have been a dry dwelling inside, or hounds would have suffered badly and would not have been fit for work.

Gordon Stagg, the former Whipper-in to Irving, told me of heavy metal chains that were hung from trees behind the farm that were used for hauling up fallen stock for hanging (meat was often hung for several days before being fed to hounds), skinning and butchering. This was used as feed for hounds and would have been most welcome as funds were not exactly abundant before Willie's time. Gordon says that the rusting chains were still up there till recent years, and he reports they could very well still be there today. I photographed the spot for this book, in company with Maud and Pearl, Willie's daughters, but alas we didn't have time to go in search of those chains. I can well imagine they are still there, hanging from the stretched-out branches, swinging to and fro in strong winds as a testimony that hounds were once kennelled here, when the hunt staff milled about busily caring for their charges and preparing for the next hunting day.

Banks' farm at Highpark, at the foot of Melbreak and the top end of Crummock Water, is where the old kennels were situated and this former farm is now a holiday let, a very charming one at that with a history rich in hunting connections. Jonathan Banks not only hunted the Melbreak Hounds for several seasons, but he also hunted with the Egremont crew who were responsible for creating many of the early strains of both unregistered and pedigree Lakeland terriers, working their stock on all large quarry, including badger and otter. Jonathan Banks, I can state with certainty, is the reason why the Melbreak had classy working terriers serving with them

The Banks' farm at High Park, at the foot of Melbreak Fell, home to the old kennels.

LEFT: *Jonathan Banks, one-time Huntsman of the Melbreak, and his family.*
RIGHT: *Annie Banks, avid hunt supporter and unofficial kennel assistant.*

even before the time of William Irving, for the Egremont strains were typey stock, even long before the 1920s and records prove that the Melbreak hunt had classy red, hard-coated terriers even as early as the 19th century.

New kennels were needed, however, as Banks was getting on and, sadly, would soon die (in January 1928) and it seems the farm may well have been going out of the family. A new site was found at Millar Place, below Dodd, and it took some time for the renovation and kennel buildings to be completed. However, the work was eventually accomplished and Willie and his wife, together with their first child, Maud, who was still a baby, moved into their new home at Millar Place from where Willie began the new season of 1928/29. It seems they moved in during the summer of 1928 and there they would enjoy many happy years together.

One Annie Banks had also moved with them, from her family farm. She was either the sister or daughter, of Jonathan Banks and was as keen a Melbreak supporter as could be found. She took up residence at the other cottage situated at the farm, a residence which is still owned by the hunt today. Annie was a great help to Willie, assisting with kennel duties and helping out as much as possible on hunting days too, despite her advancing years.

Jonathan Banks had become too old to farm by now and was possibly ill, so it was essential that new kennels be found. Also, the old place, looking it over as I have, was not entirely suited for the purpose of kennelling hounds, so Willie must have been on the look-out for new kennels. His daughter Maud has recently found records of the sale of Millar Place, the farm was owned by a Mr Towers who put the place up for public sale through Mitchell's Auctioneers on Monday September 27th 1926 at 3pm and the Melbreak committee were successful in their bidding.

1930/31 SEASON

Willie Irving took up his duties at the hunt, which often began with gathering hounds and terriers in from their walks (the families who were looking after them off-season), on **September 13th** and he also saw the appointment of a new professional Whipper-in who took up his duties on **September 20th**, just before hunting began. Albert

LEFT: *Old kennel building at High Park.* RIGHT: *High Thrushbank today.*

A young Maud, Willie's daughter, with her Lakeland terriers.

Thomas, who became a firm family friend, was Willie's new Whipper-in at the Melbreak and he was a keen young lad who was willing to learn. He had undoubtedly grown up surrounded by hounds, terriers and fell hunting, so he would already have known much of what was expected of him.

The first meet was **September 23rd** and a fox was accounted for on Whinlatter Road after a good hunt which set off from Thornthwaite Young Wood.

September 30th proved to be a good day and a fox was roused after drawing Rannerdale. Hounds then had a good hunt round White-less, across to Grasmoor and on to Eel Crags. Reynard was not tired yet, however, and made for Addacombe Hole, a spot marked on the ordnance survey map where he went to ground. Willie sent Merry and Felix to bolt their quarry, but Charlie remained below and paid the price in full, as he was worried by the terriers among the rocks.

It was on **October 2nd** that a fox was accounted for at Buttermere Lake, in the water by the shore, after a rattling hunt from Ling Crag, Red Pike, High Stile, then down into the low country. **October 16th** witnessed the official opening meet that year and hounds had a very good four-hour hunt, which never took them very far away, remaining in the Lorton Vale area for the duration. Charlie crept to ground in the end, at Red How Wood, a place that features much in the Melbreak's hunting history, but was quickly bolted. Reynard then gave hounds a good run, but was finally run into at Latterhead Farm byre.

October 18th was a very hard day for Willie and his pack. They met at Carling Knott and crossed to Melbreak where they enjoyed a hunt that saw Reynard go to ground at Mowdy Crags, where he was worried below by the terriers. Two more foxes were soon afoot, but Irving was forced to call hounds off at 3pm as it was obvious hounds weren't going to account for either fox and it was getting late in the day, with a slowly fading light.

November 15th saw hounds confined to kennels as a dense mist and storms prevented any kind of hunting, even in the low country.

December 17th witnessed a short hunt that ended with Reynard going to ground, after a meet at Cockermouth. Reynard refused to bolt, however, and so Willie, as usual, dug to his terriers, which had worried their foe by the time he reached them. It was a very old dog fox over twenty pounds in weight.

December 18th was another good day and they found at Higham, after drawing for some time, with the pack splitting in two. The first fox crossed the river and Willie used this barrier to catch them up and stop them, bringing them all back to the second fox that was being hunted by the fell hound Mountain alone. The rest of the pack now joined in the cry and they ran their quarry in at Dunthwaite Breast. Irving put in a brace of terriers, but again no fox bolted and so it was quickly worried below. They dug it out, however, and discovered that the earth dogs had accounted for an old dog fox.

December 26th was the traditional Boxing Day meet, but hounds were not loosed because of bad weather, hunting on Saturday instead. Hounds split as was often the case and the main pack had a good, but slow hunt out on the high fells at Grasmoor and Hobcarton, still going till after dark with the result not known. Nine hounds put up a lame fox on Dodd and they managed to keep it in view until they ran it down just above the fell wall where cultivated pastures met the wild mountain landscape. Charlie may have been wounded by a gamekeeper out shooting, or possibly he had been hit by a motor vehicle.

The **New Year's Day** meet witnessed hounds rousing a fox from Red How Wood and hunting it across the vale country and out onto Whiteside and Grasmoor, giving a very good hunt until it was finally lost in the low country of Littlethwaite. Willie records that the "Eskdale hounds killed in Buttermere Lake same day."

The Melbreak pack met at Cockermouth Castle on **January 15th** and they enjoyed a superb hunt from Victoria Park, which took hounds across the river Derwent and then proceeded to give them a very long run into West Cumberland Hounds country where Reynard eventually went to earth inside a drain at Isel Gate. Being in another hunt country Willie decided to do the right thing and left it to ground unmolested.

The **January 22nd** meet was at Watering Wood and they had a find at Beck Head Moss. A good hunt followed to Low Fell, Melbreak Fell and then onto the heights of Carling Knott. It seems hounds may have split on two foxes at some time during this hunt, for three hounds then went on to take their fox down to Buttermere where they killed, while another fox was run to earth on Burnbank. Stan Mawson blocked Charlie in, this being late in the day, and they returned with terriers the next day in order to deal with their fox, but it had managed to dig itself out during the long winter night. One can imagine Mawson getting quite a bit of stick from Irving for not doing a proper job of it!

There was quite a lot of snow throughout February and some hard frost into early March, which interfered with the hunting. Lamplugh

Village was the setting for a meet on **March 20th** and hounds split once again. One lot of hounds went by Red Pike and were then lost from view for some time, the result not being known. The others holed a fox at Black Crag and Tommy Swinburn's young terrier succeeded in bolting it, but it finally ran hounds off and so retained its brush.

On **March 28th** hounds roused a fox on Carling Knott and they crossed to Low fell. The pack kept with their quarry, but were struggling with the line at Beech Hill because a cur dog ran their fox and killed it before hounds reached the spot.

Some excellent hunting was enjoyed after a meet at Mockerkin Village on **April 14th** and they found almost immediately. They hunted all the way to Gillerthwaite and to Side Wood, where they killed after a good run. They then got mixed with the Eskdale hounds which were running a fox and the Melbreak hounds then hunted with them all the way to Gatesgarth where a kill was finally effected above this spot. A few hounds had got onto yet another fox and they finally ran out of scent late in the day back at Gillerthwaite. The hounds, meandering as they do, must have covered at least twenty miles and the hunt servants and followers also must have covered a lot of ground that day.

April 18th saw three inches of snow out on the bleak tops of Grasmoor and surrounding fells and, in such adverse conditions, hounds failed to find.

The pack met at Lamplugh Village Green on **April 25th** and Willie dug out a twenty-four and a half pound badger above Lamplugh Hall. Not that he was after badgers. He was employed to control foxes, but it is likely hounds marked the earth and Willie had put in one of his terriers, any of which were renowned stayers, so he would have had no choice but to dig his terrier out of that place as soon as possible, even knowing that a badger, and not a fox, was at home. They moved on after reaching terrier and badger and hounds marked again at Middle Fell. The terriers were entered and another dig ensued, during which

a fox bolted, taking hounds down to Ennerdale on a fast hunt that
ended with the result unknown. However, five cubs were dug out of
that earth and it seems from the account that there may have been
some lamb-worrying going on in that area at the time. Willie never
disturbed cubs if he could help it but lamb-worrying was probably
the reason he was in that area in the first place.

April 30th was definitely a lamb-worrying call and quite a few had
been killed. A number of shepherds were having problems and so
Willie took one lot of hounds, while Albert Thomas, the Whipper-
in, took the others. Irving hunted down into Buttermere with his
pack, but only poor scent could be found and they didn't do much.
Meanwhile Albert had a hunt on Whiteside, but failed to kill. The
elements are against hunting with hounds at this time of year when dry
and warm conditions make scent very poor and difficult to own.

Much of early May was spent trying to catch up with lamb-worrying
foxes, but very dry and warm conditions made scenting impossible.
Even so, maybe because Willie harassed the local foxes down in the
Buttermere Valley so much, the troubles had ended by May 9th and
the summer off-season began.

Hounds had enjoyed some wonderful hunts, but bad weather
had been a key feature of that season and so only thirty adult foxes
had been killed, with a few cubs taken during springtime hunting. It
has to be remembered though, that several hunts ended with hounds
going to far distant places after leaving hunt staff and followers far in
the rear and so, each season, some days go down as 'result unknown'. A
carcass was sometimes found a day or two later, usually by a shepherd
or a gamekeeper, and the kill reported. But some kills will inevitably
have gone unreported and often a fox was killed by the hounds in an
isolated spot where its carcass was safe from discovery.

CHAPTER 5

Turk of Melbreak

It was in the early days of 1930 that Willie Irving bred one of the gamest and most typey of terriers to ever serve at a fell pack, or at any other pack of hounds for that matter. Turk of Melbreak was one of the 'new' breed of Lakeland terrier and he was born on January 30th 1930 after Willie had put Rex of Melbreak to his bitch, Nettle.

Turk was registered with the Kennel Club on August 6th 1931 and his line was illustrious to say the least. Rex was bred out of Old Riff and Floss, which Irving had used with the Eskdale and Ennerdale pack when he served as part-time Whipper-in, part-time farmer to Willie Porter. Riff was in turn bred out of Jack, a Blencathra Foxhounds' terrier undoubtedly bred out of Jim Dalton lines that went back to *his* famous Turk, one of the founding sires of the pedigree Lakeland and ancestor of most unregistered stock today, and Rose, a bitch from the old Eskdale and Ennerdale lines. Rose was out of Brant and Maud, Willie's first pair of terriers which he obtained from the old breeding probably from Will Porter. It isn't known exactly how Floss was bred, though it is a certainty that she came from similar breeding stock (*see* Appendix 5). Nettle, it seems, had served at the West Cumberland Otterhounds with 'Doggy' Robinson during the summer, though she was definitely owned by Irving and may well have been bred by him.

This breeding had in its lines the terriers of Tommy Dobson, Willie Tyson, Willie Porter, Will Ritson and Thomas Rawling and they were some of the gamest in the world. They were noted for being hard-coated, rather than having the long and soft furnishings of Bedlington terriers that had characterised Lakeland terriers at that time and this attracted Irving for the simple reason that he had owned Bedlington blooded stock which had suffered very badly when out in

Willie Irving with Turk of Melbreak in 1931.

bad weather. Bad weather in the fell country means arctic conditions and the coat was so important to the early Lakeland terrier breeders. Willie Tyson was noted for producing harsh-coated stock and Willie Irving would later become noted for exactly the same reason. John Cowen, a terrierman who hunted with Irving and who continues to breed stock descended from Willie's stuff, states that Willie always bred a good coat on a terrier and they were also noted for having good heads and bone structure. This tried and tested line had served with the Eskdale and Ennerdale packs (they amalgamated in 1895) for decades and they had satisfied the needs of some of the keenest hunters Lakeland or indeed the whole country has ever produced, so Irving chose well and took really good stock with him when he took up his post at the Melbreak.

Tommy Dobson's breeding is shrouded in mystery, but it is likely that it carried the bloodlines of earth dogs from different parts of the Lake District. Dobson had hunted with and possibly Whipped-in to, Bobby Troughton of the Kendal and District Otterhounds during the late 1840s and this Huntsman was noteworthy for producing game terriers that served with this hunt. Some were coloured, others were white, but they were generally of good type and good bone structure, some of them having superb heads that would easily fit into a group of white Lakelands today, especially those bred by Gary Middleton of Kendal. Dobson would surely have owned terriers from Troughton's strain which, I believe, were infused with early fox terrier blood that had gained quite a stronghold in the north. Dobson's strain often produced whites and this colouring may have had its origins in the dogs of Bobby Troughton.

Tommy also lived near Keswick for a time and this area was noted for fell hunting and for producing Bedlington-blooded fell terriers, so undoubtedly Tommy brought into his line dogs from such breeding, before finally settling at Eskdale during the 1850s. And from then on dogs from Tyson and Ritson would have had an impact on Dobson's strain, as these were some of the gamest and hardiest stock to be found in West Cumberland in his day. It can be said with a great degree of certainty that Willie Irving's famous Turk carried in his illustrious bloodlines the dogs of such breeders, all the way back to the quality earth dogs produced by Bobby Troughton who used his stock with both otterhounds and foxhounds.

Turk entered to fox (started hunting) early and quickly established himself as one of the gamest terriers serving with a Lakeland pack of hounds. A very hard dog, he could kill foxes eagerly and with sense, but his willingness to fight underground made him not suited to badger digging which was popular at the time and considered a legitimate means of pest control, as badgers do take lambs, chickens and pheasant when opportunity arises. Turk also served with otterhounds during the summer, when Willie followed the Cockermouth and West Cumberland Otterhounds, as well as the famous Dumfriesshire pack, as often as possible and used his terriers when invited to do so. He became such a good worker in fact, that Willie used Turk whenever he needed a youngster to be taught its trade. A young terrier learns much by watching an experienced adult terrier at work and Turk became Irving's best at that time.

Many legends and myths have surrounded this dog bred by Irving in 1930 and he is still talked about to this day. One of the myths is that Turk was a great fighter, able to kill any dog or bitch that upset him. Nothing could be further from the truth. Turk was not in the least quarrelsome unless roused by another and easily fitted into kennel life, being comfortable in the company of either hounds, or other terriers. Concrete evidence that Turk was very good-natured, even with male terriers, is the fact that Willie would put young male terriers to ground alongside him. If Turk had been in any way aggressive, then Willie would not have put even a bitch to ground with this dog. So stories of him being a great fighter are untrue, unless they are with regard to foxes. He was indeed a great fighter against foxes and could finish his foe without too much fuss. By the time the 1930/31 season had ended Turk had already become a 'made' worker (a proven, hard dog not afraid to attack a fox below ground) and the summer off-season of 1931 would witness him becoming a champion show dog several times over, though not at Kennel Club shows. These were Lakeland Terrier Association shows and Turk won all over the place that summer and he also served numerous bitches. His offspring literally saturated pedigree Lakeland terrier bloodlines during 1931 and

1932 and he also sired many unregistered working terriers too. It was at this time that breeder Noney Fleming reported that Turk had won the gold medal for Best Working Terrier; and Trinket, belonging to Douglas Paisley and his wife, won the gold medal for bitches.

All of the top kennels of the time had offspring bred from Turk, including Mrs Spence, Paisley, Meagean, Gibbons and Alf Johnston. Turk proved almost unbeatable at LTA shows and, what is more important, he served regularly with the Melbreak and with otter-hounds when occasion arose, so all of the top breeders would gladly use such skilled blood on their stock. What exactly happened to Turk in the end has also been surrounded in myth and legend and tales abound of a kennel fight in which Turk met his end. Brian Plummer, in his book *The Fell Terrier* (see interview with G.H. Long), states that Turk was eventually killed in a kennel fight and this seemed conclusive, but it has now proved to be yet another myth. Thanks to Willie's diary we now know exactly what happened to him and his demise was truly tragic (see 1932/33 season).

What we also know is that Irving regarded Turk as his best ever terrier: not just for his looks and success in the show ring; but also because of his abilities in the hunting field. Such abilities were celebrated throughout the Melbreak country, for it was reported at that time that Turk could shift many a fox that had got the better of other terriers by getting itself a grand vantage point from where it could repel most attacks. In such situations Turk was always sent for and he invariably succeeded in either bolting or killing his opponent. He was a finder, a stayer and a dog that could finish a reluctant fox that had got itself into a commanding position deep inside a borran earth. He was hard-coated and narrow enough to get almost anywhere. Turk was also a prolific sire of quality stock that would both look and work very well indeed and this was another reason why Willie rated him so highly and talked fondly of this dog for the rest of his days.

Turk was such a famous dog, in fact, that an article even appeared in a Cumbrian newspaper about him. Terriers were not often named in those days in hunting reports, so Turk must have been something very special for a correspondent to focus on him in such a manner. The newspaper and correspondent are not named but he travelled

Willie (fourth from right), followers and hounds somewhere near Whinlatter in the 1930s.

north of Carlisle to have supper at Irithington village farm in early January 1938 and whilst there a Lakeland terrier of obvious quality yawned, stretched himself and then jumped to the floor from the comfortable kitchen settle where he had enjoyed a lengthy snooze. The correspondent asked about the origin of the terrier and he was told that the dog was a full-litter brother to Irving's famous Turk but had been sold by the Melbreak Huntsman because of his poor colour. The writer of the report then goes on to assure Will Irving that the terrier was enjoying a good home and was kept occupied by ridding the farm of rats (and no doubt cats as well!), and that his adventures at hunting such wily quarry also took him into the village where this game little dog had wiped out the entire local rat population, much to the villagers' delight. He doesn't state if the dog worked fox, though I suspect he would have shifted one or two from around the farm and may also have been used with the Cumberland hounds.

The new Melbreak season began on Monday **September 28th**, but it wasn't until **October 5th** that any decent hunting took place, due to summer-like conditions. They met at Stockhow Hall and ran a fox out from Frizington Parks, which they later killed. They had another good hunt and killed at Baines Quarry. The first carcass wasn't found that day and when it was discovered a day or so later it proved to be an old vixen.

On **October 21st** hounds met at Cockermouth and a fox was soon away on the outskirts of the town, later to be killed at the big rabbit warren. Irving reports that the area was "alive with foxes", but still he managed to get the pack settled on another and they eventually accounted for it in a cottage doorway at Embleton after an exciting hunt.

October 26th saw a fox flushed from Clint's Wood, Lorton, and it quickly went to ground inside a drain close to the river Cocker. Willie was soon up with his terriers and he entered one, which bolted Reynard soon afterwards. Scent was poor that day and a slow hunt was had until, four-and-a-half hours later, they pulled down their fox above the Rising Sun.

Early November witnessed some heavy flooding that stopped hunting for a day or two and it wasn't until **December 1st** that they had another notable day. Hounds drew Carling Knott and dragged out to Tarn Crags at Floutern, where they at last had Charlie afoot. He fairly flew across the fells and went out to the Red Pike district, before returning to Scaw and getting to earth among a rocky stronghold. Boss and Tiny, two terriers born earlier that same year, were entered and this may have been the first fox this pair saw. They did good work for a pair of youngsters and quickly worried their fox underground.

The Melbreak met at Scalehill on **December 26th** and it was a very misty day. Hounds got away on a fox but, Willie says, "We could see nothing." Two foxes evidently got up in front of hounds and Cora ran one on entirely her own, giving the best hunt of the day as she took it round Coledale Hause and onto Grasmoor. Reynard then took her over Whiteside and Cora killed on her own on Dodd, not far from the kennels. What a performance for a single hound!

January 5th saw hounds meet at Dean School and they had a short run with a fox at Outgang where it holed in an old drift mine (sideways shaft). The terriers were put in, but the digging team couldn't get their fox out. It was worried below. The workers couldn't reach it but they got out of there a twenty seven and a half pound sow badger instead, which the terriers had turned their attention to after killing their fox.

January 7th witnessed a long six hour hunt that began after a meet at Deanscales and ended with a kill at Red How Wood. Willie describes this as "a great hunt" and one can only read his account with envy.

Hounds drew Melbreak Fell on **January 26th** and the pack immediately split on two foxes. One lot took their fox out to The Steeple, while the others ran their foe to ground at Brunt Bield. It seems Willie was with the first lot of hounds, for terrierman Alan Nelson, a Buttermere farmer, eventually reached the bield, but hounds had left after waiting some time for someone to arrive with terriers.

Alan put in his terrier anyway, hoping to account for the fox underground, but it bolted and ran away unmolested across the bleak fell tops. It was some time after this that, whilst digging a terrier and fox out of Brunt Bield, Alan's false teeth slipped out of his mouth and fell in among the rocky depths, never to be seen again.

March 1st witnessed some very early lamb-worrying in the low country at Lorton Bottoms, at New House, and they dragged out to Low Fell where they enjoyed a good hunt. Reynard took them out to Carling Knott and then across to the heights of Melbreak Fell, but they struggled with scent as the day wore on and so finally lost their fox. It seems the worrying ended, however, as Willie did not have to go back to the area again that season.

March 3rd was memorable for the fact that hounds got mixed up with the Eskdale and Ennerdale once more, after having several foxes afoot in the Carling Knott district, but they failed to kill.

It was on **April 22nd** that they hunted the Mosedale district and they soon had a fox running, which took them on a fast hunt round Hen Combe, Black Crag, Banks, Bar Yeat and back around Carling Knott and to Blake Fell where Charlie went to ground under Black Crag at a desolate spot right out on the high tops – yet another rocky strong-hold. It took a while, but Willie was eventually up with hounds as they marked eagerly, knowing reinforcements were now on the scene, and he entered his best worker, Turk, alongside Boss, the youngster still learning his trade. Turk and Boss then quickly worried their fox, who was unwilling to face hounds again and resolutely refused to bolt. It would have been better off bolting, as it would have stood a chance out in the open, but with Turk in that earth, along with a very promising young entry, it didn't stand a chance and paid the price in full.

April 29th was when Tramp and Rex worried a livestock-killing fox which was found to be full of lamb; and another was accounted for on **May 3rd**. On **May 9th** Willie dug some cubs out of Gasgale Ghyll after worrying had taken place in the vicinity and he accounted for a fine dog fox on **May 11th** after yet more worrying.

The last day of hunting for lamb-worrying foxes in and around this area was **May 18th** and Willie dug out some cubs from an earth at Hundith Hill Woods, accounting for three but managing to save one from the terriers. Then he had a very late-call on **May 28th** and killed, which gave him a total of forty-three for that season, with a number of cubs also taken in order to stop lamb-worrying.

Turk of Melbreak had become a legend by the end of the 1931/32 season during which he had proved he could both find and kill a fox single-handed. He was used extensively at stud because of his working ability and looks and one of his best puppies was Roamer, who also won well at shows and became a very reliable worker too. Tinker was also of his getting and yet another sound worker Willie could rely on when a fox had gone to earth and needed to be bolted, or accounted for below. Turk then went on to found a dynasty and many were his descendants, including Old Flip and Mick of Millar Place.

Many of the Oregill, Kinniside, Bowderstone and Mockerkin-strain Lakeland terriers were also descended from Turk as most top breeders used his line during the 1930s when he himself, his sons and his grandsons were standing at stud. He was a truly remarkable dog and must go down in history as possibly *the* most important stud in both fell and Lakeland terrier breeding. Sid Wilkinson, John Cowen, Cyril Tyson, Gary Middleton, Arthur Irving, Harry Irving, 'Doggy' Robinson, Jack and Frank Pepper, Alf Johnston, Mrs Spence, Bob Gibbons, the Paisley brothers, Thomas Rawling, Jack Moore, G.H. Long, Bob Gibbons and a whole host of other noted breeders all used dogs that could be traced back to Irving's famous Turk of Melbreak.

Having just mentioned Old Flip I think it expedient to tell of a recent discovery that is most interesting indeed. In my book, *The Lakeland Terrier* (published by *Swan Hill Press* 2007) I wrote that I believed Jim Fleming's famous and much sought-after strain of Lakeland terrier was descended from Irving's strain and that it would go back to his Turk. The reason for this was that Fleming was a friend of Willie's and was also related to him, as Jim also married a Tyson of Ennerdale. Maud and Pearl Irving also believed that their father had bred dogs for Fleming, though they couldn't be absolutely certain of this. Fleming's strain was polished and sometimes very typey, showing a distinct link to early pedigree stuff. I am glad to say that Pearl has just handed over some pedigrees I had not previously seen and in amongst these papers was irrefutable proof of my theory.

Turk of Melbreak was put to Venus ('pet' name Tess) and from this union came Tinker. A dog known as Deepdale Holloa was then put to Gypsy of Melbreak and this mating produced yet another Tess. Deepdale Holloa was owned by Hogarth before Willie bought him, but the dog was in fact bred by Joe Wilkinson who hunted with the

Ullswater Foxhounds and later became their Whipper-in. Holloa was out of Stockbeck Sam and Wilkinson's Nettle, a bitch that served regularly with the Ullswater and she became one of the best the hunt had during the 30s, being a great finder and one that could bolt reluctant foxes. Tinker and Tess were then put together and this union produced one of *the* most famous of all working Lakeland terriers, a bitch referred to even now as Fleming's Myrt. Myrt served at the Ullswater with Anthony Barker during the Second World War and she produced many litters of puppies and went on to have a massive impact on future breeding programmes at hunts throughout the Lakes. Brian Plummer considered her to be the 'Magna Mater' of modern stock and one of *the* most important of all fell and Lakeland terriers.

Simply put, Myrt can be more accurately described as Willie Irving's Myrt, for it was he who bred her and she was a grand-daughter of his Turk of Melbreak. Myrt was very dark, almost black, and she produced some very dark offspring too. Myrt bred many pups, but one of her best, when put to Ullswater Pat (later to become registered as Korncrake of Kinniside after Bob Gibbons had bought the dog from either Fleming, Kitty Farrer, or Joe Wear), was Old Flip. Pat, in turn, was bred out of Wastwater Buglar and a bitch known as Black Wonder. Many of the Grasmere terriers were black and most, if not all, belonged to Fleming.

Gordon Stagg can well remember Flip and he says that he was a terror, as a few of Fleming's were, including Tear 'Em, the famous Ullswater dog that was on loan to Joe Wear for several seasons and was one of the gamest terriers ever to come out of

A 1932 photo of Maud with a Melbreak hound and Turk.

the Lakes. Tear 'Em was a son of Myrt and thus was a great grandson of Turk of Melbreak. Flip was born on April 3rd 1942 and Willie bought him and registered him with the Kennel Club in 1945, which suggests he probably purchased the dog as an adult. It is my guess that Flip served at the Ullswater under Anthony Barker for a season or so before he headed to the Melbreak and a number of bitches may well have been served by him in his former country before his move. What a discovery this is, for the breeding of Fleming stock has been shrouded in mystery for decades and has at last come to light.

Stagg tells a tale of Old Flip that demonstrates just how tough hill foxes can be. The Melbreak pack had run a fox in at a difficult spot and they had managed to dig in after Old Flip had been entered. He was a hard fox killer and had finished many before this time, but this one had got itself onto a high shelf and Flip just couldn't get a purchase on his foe, which dealt out severe punishment every time he tried. In the end, however, two hounds broke and rushed in and, being more able to reach their quarry, the hounds pulled it off the shelf and put an end to a valiant fox. Old Flip was incredibly game, though he was rather wild and unruly at times. No doubt plenty of work calmed him to some extent. It was Flip who sired Mick of Millar Place during the 1940s. Mick was born on August 8th 1943 and became one of Irving's best during his last seven seasons at the Melbreak and he was a looker too. Mick was another top-working grandson of the famous bitch Myrt, as well as his sister Tarnbank Trim, yet another grand worker. Turk of Melbreak truly had a massive impact on fell and Lakeland terrier breeding before his untimely and tragic demise.

This discovery also means that I was correct regarding my theory that Harry Hardisty's even more famous Turk was descended from Irving's dog of the same name. It is a well-known fact that Sid Hardisty bred Turk out of a bitch descended from Fleming's Myrt and I discovered, through John Cowen's valuable assistance, that 'Doggy' Robinson's big black and tan dog Mike was Turk's sire. We do not have the name of the dam of Hardisty's Turk, but a note in Irving's book may well shed light on this. Sid Hardisty stated to Brian Plummer when researching his book *The Fell Terrier* that Turk was bred out of a bitch given to him by Harry, which was descended from Fleming's Myrt. Willie made a note in December 27th 1958, or '59, it is not clear which of those two years it was, that his stud dog gave another service to a terrier at the kennels. Harry Hardisty was Huntsman of the Melbreak at that time and it is my belief that a daughter of Irving's dog may well have been the bitch given to Sid, from which Turk was bred. And I say this because Turk was such a smart and square Lakeland type, though with a borderish head, which was true of several early pedigree dogs. I cannot prove this, but there is much evidence to support this conclusion. This account also tells us that Hardisty continued to use Irving-bred stock after he took over at the hunt, even as late as the end of the 1950s.

Another Irving-bred terrier to serve under Harry was Vic, a big, but narrow, black and tan dog given to Gordon Stagg by Irving. Harry took to this terrier so much that he persuaded Gordon to leave it with him during the hunting season. I have no doubts that Harry would also have bred from Vic as this terrier was as game as they come and was narrow enough to get almost anywhere. That Harry had terriers with pedigree blood at the hunt is obvious.

Hounds had run a fox in under a big rock at Whinlatter and Hardisty entered his dog Rusty, a son of his famous Turk. However, this proved a very tight spot indeed and the terrier, though extremely game, just couldn't get up to his quarry. Harry then sent his Whipper-in back to the kennels for 'Old Tick' who was really in retirement with only a couple of teeth left in his mouth. Tick was so narrow that he got up to his fox and Reynard was swiftly bolted. It is my educated guess that Tick was bred down from either the mating of Irving's stud dog with one of Harry's bitches in the late 50s; or he was descended from Vic, the dog loaned to Hardisty by Gordon Stagg. Such narrow terriers were common at the Melbreak during Irving's time and Alan Johnston recently told me a tale of how Irving, having run a fox to ground, sent his Whip all the way back to kennels for a particularly narrow terrier after the others had failed to get.

I have no doubts that Mike was also descended from pedigree stuff (Robinson lived and hunted in West Cumbria where terrier strains were saturated with pedigree blood, especially that of terriers used at the Melbreak by Irving, Gibson, Pepper, Moore and Rawling), but we now have proof that the dam of Hardisty's Turk was indeed a descendant of Turk of Melbreak, through Myrt. Again, this is an exciting revelation as Hardisty's dog has hitherto been yet another with a mysterious background. Edmund Porter's famous Turk of the 1960s was bred out of Rags, a son of Turk and a dog belonging to Sid Hardisty, and this chocolate dog was both a looker and a superb worker, possibly being the best dog Porter has ever had serving at the Eskdale and Ennerdale pack. And so, through Hardisty's Turk, this dog was also a descendant of Irving's illustrious dog of the same name. Edmund still owns terriers that can be traced back to his top-winning dog, Turk.

1932/33 SEASON

Willie began gathering in his hounds on **September 12th** and the first meet was **September 20th**, with two foxes being hunted, one for a long time and distance, but no kill was effected.

A meet was scheduled at Hundith Hill on **September 29th**, but hounds came across a fox whilst on the way to the meet, at Cass How. It crossed to Low Fell and then re-crossed to Armaside where it kept to the woods and was reluctant to head out into the open again, which suggests it may have been a young fox. Reynard finally headed for open country after hounds harassed and chivvied him around low country woodlands and he made out to Sunny Brows and then higher still. He set his mask for Whinlatter now where the pack finally closed the gap and pulled down their quarry on the roadside, but only after it had binked on a number of occasions at every crag it came across.

It was on **October 10th** that Willie records that he *"had a disastrous day"* and one he would never forget. Major and Crummock, two of Irving's most trusted hounds, and Gyp and Turk of Melbreak, two of his best terriers, picked up some poison at Red How Wood whilst drawing through. This was undoubtedly strychnine and, thankfully, is said to be a painless, if unpleasant, death. It seems Willie didn't notice things were amiss until it was too late and his hounds and terriers had ingested too many of the toxins for anything to be done. Strychnine was used for the poisoning of moles and other agricultural pests and was usually carefully placed, but sometimes it got out into the open after being carried and dropped by a beast or bird; or a dog dug it out of a hole, and that is when such awful events occurred. Willie was devastated and his incredibly typey and good-working dog, Turk, together with other useful members of his pack, were lost forever. Thankfully Irving had used him to serve several bitches and so plenty of his offspring were available to continue the line and, as stated, his descendants are still around to this day.

Hounds met at Scale Bridge on **November 3rd** and they soon hit off a drag, which took them out onto the high tops at Burtness Combe where Charlie was finally roused from his daytime slumber. He didn't run too far, however, and ran straight for Whitecove, where Charlie got in among the rocks. Irving was soon at the spot and three terriers were entered, which tells us that this must have been a vast rocky fortress. Tiny, Tatters and Tick were sent in after their fox, but it wasn't for bolting and as a result was swiftly worried underground.

November 5th was the Quarrymen's Hunt and a good day was had by all. The pack hit off a drag at Gate Gills and it took them to Robinson Fell where Charlie was on his legs. In fact, two foxes got up before hounds and the pack split. One half went by Littleton, Bull Crags and then to Gable Crags, with Reynard finally eluding his pursuers at Step Ghyll. The other hounds had a good hunt around Robinson Fell, in and out of the crags there before it finally went to ground inside a rocky den. Boss and Tiny, out of the same litter and born in April 1931 out of Jock and Felix, were put to earth and they soon found their foe, worrying it after it refused to bolt. A fine dog fox was accounted for on **November 9th** after a long and difficult hunt of almost six hours.

November 16th saw hounds drawing Carling Knott once again and they had a very fast hunt by High Nook, over Banks, up Mosedale and on to Gale Fell. By Starling Dodd they raced and to Red Pike and High Stile. Reynard turned in by Thunder Ghyll and headed down to the low country and took to the waters of Buttermere, but was killed in the lake. E. Dixon borrowed a rowing boat and recovered the sodden carcass that had been left in the water by hounds.

November 19th witnessed hounds running a fox round by Hobcarton, Long Crag, Grisedale Pike and then over Whinlatter. Charlie then ran into a drain near Darling How and Boss and Whisk were put to ground in order to shift him. However, as was often the case, their quarry was reluctant to leave its lair and so was worried before Willie could dig it out. He uncovered a now dead old dog fox.

January 4th was not a good day for the Melbreak. They enjoyed a superb hunt that went from Low Fell and onto Carling Knott, finally running out of scent at Lamplugh Village, but poor young Cleaver got away on couples with another hound and was hanged, probably when he jumped a gate without the other hound taking the same route.

January 25th was a meet at Cockermouth Castle and they put a fox up at Victoria Park. In fact, it wasn't long before several foxes were running and causing much confusion and the hounds, not surprisingly, failed to make a kill. This often happened where there were large numbers of foxes laying scent all over the place. Willie now came across Jim Kitchen and a few others who were badger digging at Lands. He discovered that a few hounds had got away on a single fox and they had killed after crossing the river Derwent.

February 7th was the day of a meet at Mockerkin Village and hounds followed a cold drag out to Carling Knott and then split. One lot had a good hunt over Hen Combe, Gale Fell, Dodd, back by Tarn Crags and then ran their fox in at Gale Fell. Reynard bolted, but Willie viewed him going into another earth and was quickly on the spot with two of his best terriers, Boss and Whisk. Whisk was born on January 2nd 1932 and was registered with the Kennel Club on July 5th of that year under the name of Hobcarton Whisk. He was sired by Turk of Melbreak and his dam was Peggy of Melbreak who was bred by Jack Pepper and owned by Irving. Whisk was an incredibly good worker and one of the best terriers around in the 30s. He, along with Boss, entered the lair and quickly found, engaging their foe and killing it below ground in typical early Lakeland terrier fashion. Nine hounds went away after another fox to Ennerdale side and killed at Mireside garden.

March 13th saw a fox going to ground in sand holes at Winscales where it was worried by Wisp and Merry. Hounds killed another at Wythemoor.

March 21st witnessed Cracker having a lone hunt on a fox after one had been lost that had been hunted from Lamplugh. Cracker had somehow got away from the pack and had driven his quarry to a scree-bed, where it ran above the rough rocky ground, whilst Cracker shadowed it below. This incident demonstrates the intelligence of these fell hounds for, instead of trying to cross the rocks, Cracker ran parallel with his foe and then he followed it as it descended Low Fell, making for the low country and no doubt hoping to reach the high mountains across the valley. By the time Reynard reached the bottoms, Cracker, having kept parallel with it, wasn't far behind and he soon ran it down alone and unaided, coursing it on level ground.

March 27th witnessed a fast hunt, despite warm and dry conditions, with the fox finally going to earth at Wythop Hall Fell after travelling quite some distance. Whisk was on hand again and Willie put him in. He soon found his quarry and engaged it, but it wouldn't bolt and so an old dog fox had been worried by the time Whisk was dug out. **April 8th** was a memorable day and a good hunt was had on Low Fell, Red How Wood, Rogerscale, back by High Mosser, Pardshaw and to High Dyke, with Charlie finally being caught in a byre at Southwaite.

April 14th was the traditional Good Friday meet at Buttermere and what a cracker it was. Hounds had a fox away after hitting off a

The end of a successful hunt. Those who hunted with Willie Irving recalled that he had an extraordinary knack of anticipating the movements of his quarry, nearly always being in at the kill.

drag in glorious sunshine close to Buttermere Hotel and a 'girt big un' was unkennelled at Gate Ghylls. They then had a fast hunt and Reynard skirted the hamlet and climbed out for Newland Hause, round Robinson, Littleton, Gable crag and on to Eel Crags, where the glorious swell of music could be heard from afar. Reynard now took them to Maiden Moor and in past Littleton, back up Newlands Bottom and then went to ground at Blea Crag, inside a large rock den. Willie was on the spot after hounds had been marking wildly for a time and there put Peggy and Mist to ground. This Peggy was bred by Pepper on August 6th 1930 and registered by Willie on June 20th 1932. She was bred out of Nip and Peggy and was a wonderful worker. The brace of earth dogs, after what was reportedly a grim battle, worried their fox below and they then drew the carcass of a large dog fox out of that rocky lair, which saved much digging. This was a very welcome end too, for it had taken place in a noted bad place that couldn't really be dug without risk.

It was on **April 28th** that Willie headed for Buttermere in response to several complaints of lamb-worrying and Mr and Mrs Hind kindly put them up, as they often did. A start was made at daybreak next morning close to Buttermere Hotel and a warm drag was almost instantly picked up by the eager pack. Reynard was soon viewed away close to Gate Gills and he went like the wind sweeping off the Russian Steppes. He raced away by Kirkclose and hard by Gatesgarth Farm, now going straight up the Honister valley. He made out to the right now and climbed High Rake, making for the formidable Honister Crag, which must have filled Willie and Albert with dread, as hounds are always in great danger in such country. He traversed Brunt Scarf and made for the quarries at Dubs, though he kept out of the rockpiles there. Charlie was next viewed coming in at Warnscales and then made over the rough and boulder-strewn country below and about Raven Crag. He then doubled back and made up Fleetwith side and the going was rough indeed as he crossed over Honister. He kept to the rocky country as much as possible, leaving plenty of 'impossible' obstacles in his wake, and then made for Yew Crags, eventually 'binking' at Buxom Hows.

One of the hounds managed to climb the dangerous rocky ledges and almost reached the fox, when it jumped out, falling seventy or eighty feet of sheer-drop down the rock face. Charlie was unharmed by the fall, however, and raced on straight down the pass. Hounds streamed down the face of the crag in a long line of white, brown and black bodies and were soon on terms with their valiant foe. Their quarry headed towards Honister Crag as they closed the gap and it seemed as though they were about to get their reward, but Reynard dived underneath a huge boulder just in time, as hounds were practically on his brush, and there he crept well away from their reach. They bayed into the rocky den eagerly, until Willie arrived soon after with his earth dogs keen to get in. It had been an incredibly fast hunt with hardly a breathing space for fox or hounds and the outcome was as yet uncertain, with such a stronghold gained by wily Reynard. However, Whisk and Wasp, incredibly game and capable tykes, were there and Willie loosed them into the earth. They soon located the skulking fox and finished him below ground as Willie dug to them. He finally reached his terriers after some back-wrenching labour, which had accounted for a fine dog fox. It was still only 7.30am!

Hounds had a very hard day on **May 6ᵗʰ** on a lamb-killing fox and they had it afoot at Scales Bridge. They went out Ruddy Beck and to

Red Pike, High Crag, Scarf Gap, Warnscales, and out Black Beck, over Honister and to Gatesgarth side. To Gate Gills now, then round Moss and in past Bowder Beck and down Scale to Melbreak and over Pillar Rake to Mosedale. They had already crossed some of the roughest country in England, but plenty more was ahead. They now headed up by Loweswater and Lanthwaite Wood and over to Whiteside, going up Cold Ghyll and onto the frowning heights of Hobcarton. They then crossed to Coledale and over Dove Crags to Grasmoor Point, going down Bannerdale Side to Lad Hows, Rannerdale Knott, High Coppice, past Bowder Beck once more and on to Scale. Out by Ruddy Beck they coursed, and to Red Pike, thence to Burtness Close, High Crag and to Warnscales yet again, then up and over Fleetwith Pike where Reynard at last went to ground in a gryke at Brunt Scarf after an incredible *twelve hour* hunt that had covered many miles.

The terriers, unfortunately, couldn't reach their fox and so efforts were made to dig into the gryke and open up a way for them. Irving's terriers were incredibly narrow-fronted, yet even they couldn't get in, and it says something of the agility of the fox when terriers of such ilk cannot get to them. Unfortunately, there was a rush in of stone as the difficult and dangerous digging progressed and so operations had to be abandoned, with the fox left trapped below ground. Even the oldest of hunters could not remember such a grand hunt ever having taken place and Willie Irving became an even more renowned Huntsman after this day of incredible and wonderful sport.

May 12th was the final day on a lamb-worrying fox and hounds had a hunt from Rigg House, which ended when Charlie went to earth at Carling Knott and was worried below by the terriers. This finished the season with forty adult foxes killed and a few litters of cubs dug out during lamb-worrying calls.

CHAPTER 6

A Portrait of Willie Irving

There were some hardened followers of the Melbreak and it was reported by reliable eyewitnesses that Jonathan Banks was among the best of them. He hunted hounds from 1865 to 1917 after taking over from Will Sharp and no doubt after having whipped-in to him. Sharp had been there from around 1860. Banks liked to 'louse' his hounds and then run up Melbreak just to get his wind, before starting! Willie Irving was of a similar mould.

Willie was an Ennerdale-bred lad and it was said that he played truant from school to follow hounds and one can well believe this to be true. His knowledge of the fox made him a naturalist and he knew every inch of those fells from sheep farming, following hounds and fell running during his early life. And, most importantly, he was a tireless walker who had a long 'raking' stride that was nigh-on impossible to keep with. Many tried and failed.

His reputation was one of 'an ideal Huntsman' and his stamina and endurance made him a legend, but so did his knowledge of the chase and of the wily nature of the prey he hunted. For it was said, again by those who knew and hunted regularly with him, that he had a knack of anticipating the movements of his quarry, often being in at the kill and not too far away whenever Charlie went to ground, which was quite often. He was also well-versed in ailments affecting his hounds and terriers and he had a reputation for always keeping them in good order and treating them thoroughly after a day's hunting if they had picked up injuries. It was also reported that he was 'the soul of geniality' and was immensely popular with the large Melbreak following 'from Keswick to Whitehaven'. The farmers throughout the country gave solid support to the Melbreak Foxhounds and they supported Willie in particular, who, being of farming stock himself, could talk their language and genuinely sympathise with their problems. 'An ideal Huntsman' are words any man would be glad to be known by and such statements prove that Willie did a great job at the hunt, not only controlling foxes with great effect and enthusiasm, but also liaising with villagers and farmers alike and inspiring much support from his community.

He was a great organiser too and he carried out his hunting according to this quality. Meets had to be well organised with Willie and he hated too much 'hollering' of foxes, preferring to allow hounds to work independently of man as much as possible, for he had seen too many hunts ruined by people shouting and waving on the fells. At earths he strictly forbade noise of any kind and would wait patiently for the terriers to find and bolt their fox. If there was a large following and Reynard wouldn't bolt, then Willie would move his hounds on and try for another, leaving reliable followers at the earth. But if few followers were out he would always be there at the head of any dig, until terrier and fox were uncovered. Many hunts ended with a dig and hounds had to wait patiently until their Huntsman had finished. And then it was usually back to kennels in order to feed, bed down and treat hounds and terriers, then on to an Inn where celebrations were held.

Willie was also a kind and caring man and he did his utmost to look after older followers who had given lifelong support to the Melbreak. When they became too old and frail to hunt anymore, or were ill for any length of time, he would visit them and keep them informed of events. No doubt a glass or two was passed round and much reminiscing enjoyed on these occasions!

John Cowen tells an interesting tale of a time when Hardisty was hunting hounds. The pack had run a fox in up on the fells and Cowen was doing the terrier work at the time. Willie Irving, enjoying his retirement, was also out that day and he arrived at the scene just as John put in his terrier. Cowen was then wandering around trying to find his terrier, as it had now been gone for some time. Irving joined him in the search, but a big chap, a bit of a loud-mouth, was making an 'ell of a din' and so Willie rounded on the chap and glared into his face, warning him to 'shut it' and 'keep quiet' while they searched for any sound of the terrier. Willie couldn't stand disruption and bad organisation of any sort and, though normally friendly and easy to get on with, was plainly not one to be crossed. The big chap slunk into the background and did as he was told!

1933/34 SEASON

The first meet was **September 20th**, but, though there were plenty of foxes around, conditions were warm and dry and no scent held.

On **October 2nd** the pack hit off a drag at Lanthwaite Wood and went out by Red Ghyll and had it away, hunting over the tops of Grasmoor and back down to Lanthwaite fields. Reynard then climbed out again, up Whiteside and Gasgale Crags and round to Boat Crag. He took a similar round once more and then holed near Boat Crag. It seems hunters had stuck to the tops and so Willie was soon on hand with a brace of terriers, Tramp and Roamer. Many accuse pedigree stock of being bad fighters amongst each other, but here again we have Irving putting two dogs to ground at the same time, which tells us just how unlikely they were to fight with one another.

I am not certain of the breeding of Tramp, but it is likely he was a litter brother to Turk of Melbreak. Roamer, however, is well known to us and he was a son of Turk of Melbreak, out of Peggy of Melbreak and was born August 15th 1932. He was bred exactly as was Whisk, but from a litter born seven or so months later. Roamer was registered with the Kennel Club on February 14th 1933. The pair found their quarry skulking among the rocks and a tussle ensued, whilst Willie dug down. He soon uncovered his terriers, which had finished a fine young dog fox.

October 12th was the opening meet at Kirkstile and there was a large turn-out to see a fox roused from Watering Wood, which went in a drain at Rogerscale, only to be worried by Ruffler and Peggy. Willie dug it out and it proved to be an old dog fox. **October 14th** witnessed yet another hunt coming to a conclusion when Reynard

Willie Irving with the Melbreak hounds and terriers at Crummock Water on Good Friday, 1934 or 1936.

went to ground at Dodd. Jewel and Ruffler were entered and set about worrying their quarry, which wouldn't bolt. This bitch was Jewel of Loweswater and she was a litter sister of Roamer and a very useful bitch. Willie took many foxes with this famous Melbreak pedigree Lakeland terrier.

October 17th saw a fox run in at Armaside Fell and this was worried below ground by brother and sister, Jewel and Roamer. A second fox was taken above ground near Gasgale Ghyll.

October 31st witnessed hounds hunting the Cockermouth district where they were usually kennelled for the week. Hounds enjoyed a good hunt in the woods about Cockermouth and no doubt their glorious music could be heard echoing among the trees back in the town itself as they had their quarry away to Higham and Lowfield, where it holed inside a drain. Some of these drains were deep and quite dangerous and Whisk was put in. He found after quite a search and engaged his foe, but it wouldn't bolt and so this son of Turk, after a hard tussle, worried his fox in the darkness below.

November 7th was a day when hounds split yet again. The first lot went out by Pillar Rake and Mowdy Crags and they holed their fox at Gale Fell, which wouldn't shift and so was worried underground by Tramp and Felix. The other hounds crossed the vale to Red How and were split again, with some still running after dark, their voices singing from the fells and valleys through the pitch-blackness of a late autumn evening. Lost hounds tend to return to their 'puppy walking' families or to the kennels alone next day.

November 18th saw hounds in the low country after a meet at Deanscales and a fox was quickly away from Lucetta Wood, which took hounds all the way back to High Lorton, not far from kennels, where too many folk interfered with hounds and spoiled the hunt. Followers would sometimes see a fox and holler, which would get the hounds over-excited or even cause them to follow a hare. Hounds are really meant to follow a trail unaided. Willie was no doubt livid and he didn't mince his words when things needed to be said.

November 21st saw hounds and hunt servants billeted at Buttermere Hotel for the week and on Tuesday hounds holed a fox that was worried below ground at Gate Ghyll. Music went on her own after a second and this was killed by cur dogs at Newlands after she had pressured it for some distance. Foxes evaded capture for the rest of that week, though some excellent hunts were enjoyed.

December 2nd was a Kirkstile meet and they found in Red How Wood, which went to Dodd immediately, then on to Watering Wood where it holed. The terrier bolted it, but it holed again soon after and was thus worried by terriers during this second stint to ground – an old dog fox. Another fox was hunted from the same place, possibly having bolted from the second earth, and this went to ground at Rogerscale inside the drain that held many foxes during Melbreak hunts. The fact that it was used so much testifies to how carefully

Irving's Melbreak pack at the Brown Cow, Cockermouth.

these fell hunters back-filled the earths they dug. Reynard wouldn't bolt and so was worried by Ruffler and Tick.

December 5th witnessed hunting being cancelled due to the funeral of a Mr Pearson, an ex-Whip to Jonathan 'Jonty' Banks, who had been a lifelong supporter of the Melbreak Foxhounds.

January 9th saw a fox roused from Ling Fell and they had a fast hunt round Sunny Brows, Armaside Fell and back to Harrot, where it holed at Cass How. Wasp and Tick were put in and they duly finished their fox underground. Wasp is certainly the ancestor of many pedigree Lakeland terriers, and although I cannot find any breeding record for this terrier, I have reason to believe that Wasp may have been bred out of Trigger of Carrow, another son of Irving's famous Turk.

January 12th witnessed a single hound run a fox all the way to Bassenthwaite where it went into the lake and sunk before the hound could get to it.

January 29th proved a hard and tiring day. Hounds found a fox skulking in Grisedale Ghyll, which then took them on all the tops between Loweswater, Braithwaite, Newlands and Buttermere, before eventually being killed in Newlands as it was getting dark, after a wonderful seven and a half hours of hunting.

February 5th witnessed a most unusual event when Reynard shot down a large pipe and was followed in there by hounds. When it emerged it was being chased around St Helen's School and was finally accounted for close to the school. This was a large and fine dog fox.

Hounds marked a fox to ground at Dunthwaite on **February 22nd** and Jewel was put in. Willie was hoping for a bolt, but most Lakeland terriers of that era were capable of killing any fox that would not, or could not, shift. True to her breed, Jewel tackled her quarry and a battle royal took place, which ended with Jewel worrying her fox before she could be dug out.

March 31st saw the traditional Good Friday meet being held at Buttermere and hounds put off in Gate Gills. Willie cheered on his hounds and they quickly settled on the line, their music swelling to one loud and glorious chorus as they traversed the rough and rocky fell country, going first round Hindscarth and on now to Robinson and Knottriggs, going back out by Littleton. Another fox was away here and most hounds switched to this, being more able to own a fresh line, but Lonely and Rally stuck to their first and killed it below Littleton after quite a severe run. Maud is pretty sure this is the day Willie had his famous Crummock Water photograph taken that is seen on the cover of this book (and page 104), though the other date put forward is two years later on Good Friday 1936.

April 23rd was a lamb-worrying call, with several farmers having problems, so Willie took one lot of hounds while Albert took the rest. Albert loosed around the lowland pastures from Buttermere and a drag took them back up the valley to Dodd, where he dug out a vixen and cubs. Which terrier was used is impossible to say, but it seems that Albert often walked out with Whisk during his time as Whipper-in, so this dog may have been put to ground on this occasion. Meanwhile Willie loosed at Swinside End, but lost a fox after a good hunt at Braithwaite. He then returned to Buttermere where they hunted Wednesday, Thursday, Friday and Saturday and hounds were foot-sore after such mighty efforts to catch up with marauding foxes. Wednesday was his best outing and they enjoyed a fast hunt from Crummock Lake Head and out onto the fells by Blea Crag. On to Red Pike and to High Stile they raced, then away to Dodd. Reynard chose to go to earth at Blea Combe. Tiny and Jewel were there and Willie entered this pair of terriers, which soon put an end to any more lamb-worrying from that particular fox. Terriers killed another to ground at Low Bank on Thursday and on that same day Willie dug out a vixen and cubs at another spot nearby. They failed to find Friday and Saturday but lamb-worrying had almost ended in that district for the season.

Only one more call came in and that was on **May 2ⁿᵈ**, but they failed to kill and there were no more problems during this particular springtime.

Willie, Albert and the Melbreak pack had enjoyed a very good season and they finished with sixty-two adult foxes being accounted for and a few litters of cubs to add to the tally. It had been a very busy season for terriers too and their workload had been very demanding indeed. They were often used to chase out any foxes skulking in dense and almost impenetrable undergrowth, where hounds found it impossible to get. There were many places within the Melbreak country that contained such undergrowth and the narrow terriers were essential for working out such places. It is a good thing that Lakeland terriers have been bred to be hardy and resilient, otherwise they would not have coped with the heavy demands made upon them.

CHAPTER 7

The Melbreak Terriers

It is true to say that many of the fell pack Huntsmen, though very distinguished hound breeders and capable of getting their pack to do nigh-on anything for them, regarded what are known in the Lakes as 'laal' (little) terriers as simply a convenient tool with which to keep a hunt going, or an aid to ending the life of any fox refusing to bolt from its underground lair. Terriers do seem to have been rather an afterthought with many Huntsmen and most hunt reports do not mention the names of the little tykes sent deep below to bolt, or worry (kill) their fox, as though they were not worthy of any individual recognition. Not so with Willie Irving. His daughter Pearl states that he believed it was possible to breed a good-looking terrier that could both win at summer shows *and* work during the season and his diaries and newspaper reports prove beyond any doubt that he was correct in his thinking. His terriers were prized just as much as his hounds and in this regard he was a real credit to the hunting tradition of the Lake District. And, unlike most Huntsmen, he often recorded by name the terriers he used during hunts, though these accounts were sometimes very brief and basic because of demands on his time.

Fox terriers were abundant in the Lake District. The breed had been tested to the full on the exposed moors of Devon, Somerset and Cornwall for decades, proving useful in a variety of earths, including those found in rock. On many occasions these white-bodied terriers had been used to bolt foxes from deep rocky lairs on places such as Exmoor and Dartmoor and so the hunting folk of the fell country had few, if any, reservations about bringing these bloodlines into their own breeding programmes. Bobby Troughton certainly used fox terrier blood, as did Tommy Dobson and Jim Dalton of the Blencathra Foxhounds.

This mix of different breeds served a purpose and it wasn't just about exhibiting, as some authors claim. Willie Irving states in one of his preserved letters that most terriers of his boyhood days were Bedlington-blooded dogs and that these had poor coats. He recalled carrying semi-conscious terriers to nearby farms on several occasions in an attempt to save them after they had collapsed from exposure in severe weather conditions classed as 'arctic' in the fells. He says that their coats were soft and open and this gave little protection from the elements. Therefore many breeders chose to use fox terrier blood, as well as Irish and Welsh, to improve coat. This produced a very harsh, tight-knit jacket that kept much of the wind and rain at bay and so such stock suffered far less. True, this change in coat meant the breed improved from scruffy little tykes to something much more pleasing to the eye, but such breeding programmes were about producing more useful stock to serve with the fell packs. Dalton certainly used fox terrier blood to improve the coat and hardiness on his fell stock, which in turn produced good looking stock of excellent type, some of which would easily win at shows today. But, first and foremost, these terriers were workers and workers of the very best type. Nothing but the best could possibly hope to have served successfully with a mountain pack of hounds.

It was for such reasons that Willie changed to breeding the improved type of fell terrier and these with harsh jackets, narrow fronts and good strong heads (bull terrier had already been used to produce fox terriers and so good bone and heads were typical during the 19th and early 20th centuries) were referred to as Patterdale terriers. They were far hardier than the Bedlington type of fell terrier and were just as game, so many began keeping this Patterdale type which probably began to be bred during the early part of the 19th century, gaining in popularity, particularly in the western regions, as that century progressed. Dalton, Farrer, Rawling, Paisley, Banks, Braithwaite Wilson, Willie Tyson, Will Ritson and the Nelson family: all began keeping this type with better coats and narrow fronts and Willie Irving also abandoned the rough-and-ready shaggy terriers with poor coats and began keeping the improved strains instead. These, in 1912, were given the name of Lakeland terrier (though this name was later given to any type of coloured terrier serving at the fell packs, or with a Lakeland pack of otterhounds).

When Irving arrived at the Melbreak as Huntsman in 1926 there were already several of this improved type being used at the hunt and he brought these into his own strain, which had originated from the Eskdale and Ennerdale country. From the late 1920s onward the Melbreak country became 'swamped' with terriers from Irving's breeding programme and their influence was great throughout the whole Lakes during his time at the hunt. The resulting stock was game for certain and they would worry any fox if it did not bolt swiftly. They also engaged badger in the same manner and many suffered terrible maulings when encountering 'Brock'.

One of Willie's hunts ended in a fox going to ground in the low country and the terriers were sent in to find it. However, a badger was already at home there and the terriers turned their attention to this. Willie and his helpers dug down towards the bumps and grunts going on below and uncovered his terriers in what is termed

Richard Head and the Melbreak Hunt in Cockermouth town centre just before Willie took over.

as 'mortal combat' with 'Brock'. No doubt they had suffered badly during the encounter as badgers are incredibly tough and cannot usually be destroyed, even by a brace of terriers. Their powerful jaws inflict hard bites that can tear off the bottom jaw of a terrier, or smash the top jaw, thus killing their opponent. Rather than a terrier willing to fight a badger, what was required was a terrier who would hold a badger at bay and so crossbreds between border and Lakeland terriers were often used for digging out badgers. Pure Lakelands were used too, but usually only those that had enough sense to stand off their quarry and avoid jaw-to-jaw encounters.

1934/35 SEASON

Willie began his work for the new season on **September 15th** and the first fixture was on **September 18th** when hounds had several foxes roused at Red How Wood, with one going to ground and being accounted for using terriers near Foulsyke Wood.

October 15th was a Rigg House meet at Winscales and a fox was soon away, but it went to ground at Wythemoor Pit Wood. Charlie bolted from the terriers and he was soon killed in the open. Cora ran a second fox all by herself and killed it at Jackie Planting. A third fox was hunted that day, but it secured its own brush when hounds failed to hold the line any longer at Oldfield.

Hounds enjoyed a fast but short hunt on Ling Fell on **October 23rd** and Reynard later crept below ground and thus out of reach of the oncoming pack. This was duly worried by the terriers, but a second fox was in the same hole and this one bolted at speed, making across the open fell with hounds quickly in pursuit. This gave a fast run and headed to Chapel Wood where it went to earth once more. Followers remained with the first terriers put to ground while Willie followed his pack and soon arrived at the hole they were now keenly marking. He put in his bitch Jewel and it wasn't long before sounds from below indicated a sure find. Charlie wasn't for bolting and stayed and made a fight of it instead. This was a bad choice as it turned out, for Jewel worried her fox underground.

Another fast hunt ensued during a Cockermouth hunting week on **November 23rd** (they often stayed in Cockermouth Castle, arriving on foot) and their fox made for a hole at Andrew Bank. Willie was soon on the scene where hounds marked eagerly indeed and a terrier was entered, though he doesn't state which. However, Willie moved hounds on after Reynard wouldn't bolt and he left Jim Kitchen and one or two helpers at the earth and they dug out their fox after quite some time and effort.

The Melbreak met at Arlecdon on **January 19th** and Willie drew much of the low country before finally finding at Jackie Planting. They enjoyed a good hunt by Branthwaite and on up to Winscales where Charlie made to earth at Pit Wood. Willie came upon them marking and put in Roamer, his son of Turk. Roamer found in a short while and engaged his fox. Finding things a little too heated Charlie decided to make for open ground once more and bolted. However, the fight with Roamer had taken it out of him and he was killed after a short run.

Hounds found a fox and roused it from Forestry Woods on **January 24th** during another week of hunting at Cockermouth and a good day ensued. Reynard made tracks for Higham and ran through dense cover in an attempt to throw off hounds. It came by Bassenthwaite Lake and across the bottoms for Wythop Wood. There was much thick cover here too and Charlie made the most of it, but hounds persisted and where cover was too dense for them terriers were put in, in order to flush out their skulking quarry and keep the hunt moving. Reynard was eventually forced out by Beck Wythop and the glorious music of hounds, echoing among the woods straddling the higher fells all around, chased after their quarry as it made past the Pheasant Hotel and then went on to cross the railway. Charlie now ran 'twixt Brathay Hill and Crag Farm and then climbed the slopes to Higham. Hounds pressed their fox hard enough for it to go to ground at Silver

Ghyll and terrier Jewel was entered into this rocky lair. As was often the case after a good hunt, Reynard refused to bolt and so a battle took place that ended in Jewel worrying her fox below ground, which was dug out after strenuous efforts and proved to be a fine vixen.

Some time before this week of hunting in the Cockermouth district, one of Irving's best hounds, Cracker had gone missing during a hunt in the Workington area. He had been missing for some time and, naturally, Irving was worried about this most reliable of pack members (we will discover the outcome later in the diaries).

On **February 15th** Willie records a hunt that ended with J. Bland believing hounds had killed about Mosey Bank. This could be Jack Bland, the father of Richard 'Pritch' Bland who would hunt the Melbreak himself decades later. Jack was a great friend of Frank Pepper, who also hunted with the Melbreak, though this pair also followed the Blencathra Foxhounds whenever possible.

February 28th witnessed a meet at Greysouthen and a fox was away from Billy Wood. Reynard eventually ran to ground at Wellington. Here Crystal, one of the hounds, got into the drain and right up to

Bowderstone Cottage, the home of Jack and Frank Pepper.

her fox, where she worried it, but couldn't get out. Other hounds had also disappeared below ground, but they all returned safely, with only Crystal still missing. So a long and gruelling dig ensued: the drain was estimated to be at least six feet deep (though there was no lack of volunteers) and she was finally freed. Darkness had fallen some time before Crystal was released, but the diggers were unceasing and went on by the light of lanterns. This was quite an unusual event and was widely reported by local newspapers at the time.

March 4th saw Albert Thomas taking charge of hounds because Willie had a lame ankle and so was out of action. Hounds found a fox after drawing for a long time at Scaw Crags, but they could do hardly anything with scent and so ended a poor day.

Hounds were kennelled at Gatesgarth for a week of hunting from **March 26th** and on the Tuesday they enjoyed a superb day. Willie and Albert, along with the pack, had been put up by the Richardson family. A drag in low-lying land took hounds to Thunder Ghyll and Charlie was seen stealing away from here and a grand hunt followed, with hounds keenly speaking to a good line. Visibility in this area was good for a change and mist was thankfully non-existent. Reynard led hounds all over the place, up onto the high tops and down into the low country, then up the steep fellside again and passing Brunt Bield, rather than going into this noted stronghold. The fox made for White Cove and eventually reached Eagle Crag and crawled into a vast rock den that was more than a little difficult to work. However, Scamp and Nan were put in and they quickly found their quarry, which, for a change, bolted rather speedily. Reynard didn't get far, however, and was coursed down the rough screes, finally being rolled over below Burtness Combe by the fast oncoming pack.

April 5th was a very good day and hounds followed a drag to Red How Wood where they at last unkennelled a fox, which had taken shelter for the day in some very dense cover. Hounds got it moving in the end though, and it emerged on the banks of the river Cocker. It crossed the river and headed for Scale Hill, running left of the hotel

Sisters Pearl and Maud Irving at Millar Place, 1939.

there. Lanthwaite Woods were reached and Charlie now made across the low country for Whiteside where he climbed and crossed the steep ghyll, making out for the rough screes of Grasmoor. A second fox was up here, which distracted some hounds and the pack split, but scent ran out at Whinlatter after a good hunt. The original fox was hunted over Grasmoor and Whiteless Pike, now going through Whiteless Ghyll and on to Lad Hows, where Reynard went to ground. Willie tramped the high places and soon came upon his pack, which were marking amongst this rocky lair. Jewel and Rock were entered and a terrific waterloo broke out below ground, with an old dog fox finally being worried and then dug out. Rock is the leggy black and tan terrier at the feet of Irving in the cover photograph of this book, taken at Crummock Water in either 1934, or 1936. Rock doesn't appear in any hunts until this season and so it is likely to have been 1936 when this famous photograph was taken. Even today it still hangs on the walls of many Lakeland cottages and farmhouses, particularly within the Melbreak country.

Hounds met at the Star Inn on **April 22nd** and they found at Jackie Planting. They enjoyed a good hunt from here by Wythemoor slag banks, Gilgarran, Moorside and back to where they first found. Charlie holed at this wood and terriers were entered. They flushed a dog fox and it was got out, but the terriers had turned their attention to a large badger and were locked in combat when finally dug out. The badger weighed twenty-six pounds.

Irving's final hunt of that season was on **May 18th** and they finished with fifty-four foxes killed. They had quite a few problems with lamb-worrying and both hunt servants were kept busy trying to catch the culprits. They succeeded on quite a few occasions.

Willie Irving bred terriers in large numbers and sold many of his puppies, while others he kept, but had them 'walked' in the same manner as hounds were walked in those days. For instance, newspaper reports state that Bob Gibson used his terrier Nan on occasions when a fox was run in (i.e. to ground), but Nan was bred by and belonged to the Melbreak Huntsman. Bob Gibson obviously walked Nan for Willie during the off-season and sometimes took her with him during hunting, but she was one of Willie's favourites and Maud can remember her spending quite a bit of time in the house. Most terriers were in kennel when not at exercise, at shows, or out hunting, but Nan often came into the house and she took quite a liking to Pearl who was only a baby at the time. In fact, Nan was so fond of Pearl that she actually took to standing guard over her as she lay in her pram and woe-betide anyone, or anything, intent on harming her. Nan can be seen in the famous Crummock Water photograph (*see book jacket*) coupled to Jerry, the big dog on the far right of the picture. Nan was an extremely game bitch and she could finish a fox single-handed. She was also incredibly hardy and was once trapped to ground for several days before finally getting herself out of a tight spot due to weight loss.

Thomas Rawling was another who walked terriers for the Melbreak and he and Willie bred several together, using each-other's stud dogs and swapping pups. In fact, with such breeders it is impossible to separate bloodlines. Many of Rawling's terriers were bred out of Irving stuff and the reverse could be said of Willie's dogs. Rawling, a schoolteacher bred from Ennerdale farming stock, was a keen terrierman and his strain was used at both the Melbreak and the Eskdale and Ennerdale packs. They were also typey stock that gave rise to much of the early pedigree bloodlines. It was Rawling's Rock that founded Johnny Richardson's famous strain during the latter half of the 1930s when put to a Blencathra-bred bitch and Rock would be partly bred from Irving stuff, possibly from Turk, or Rex of Melbreak.

Jack Moore is another who walked terriers for Irving and the walking system gives much cause for confusion. When a terrier was walked by a follower of the hunt it was often said to be *their* terrier, despite the fact that it had been bred by the Huntsman, or maybe his Whipper-in, and actually belonged to the hunt. This means that unravelling pedigrees is very difficult indeed and while a terrier may be referred to as J. Moore's dog, the truth could be that it was bred and owned by Irving, but was walked by Moore. Also, many of the terriers belonging to followers were actually bred by Willie and several of these he brought back into his own strain over the years.

Old Flip, for instance, though owned and registered by Willie, was walked at a local farm and Irving could call on the dog's services at any time. Flip did quite a bit of work at the hunt and Willie used him at stud on his bitches, despite the fact that he was walked by a follower and remained with him the year round.

Pearl says that Willie took back many of the pups he sold in order to enter them to fox for their owners and this helped keep the working instinct strong in pedigree stock. It is also true to say that some of the keener and more reliable followers would be entrusted with pregnant bitches in order to assist Willie, who may have already been caring for a litter or two. Just as some reared hound pups for the Huntsman, so did some rear terrier pups, though, again, Irving was the owner and breeder of such stock.

Willie began work on **September 14th** and his first most successful outing was at Harrot on **September 20th**. Hounds had a good hunt that took in Harrot, High Side, Wythop Moss, Sunny Brows and Darling How where Reynard holed in a drain. Willie eventually reached the spot and put in Whisk, who was shaping up to be one of the best terriers working with a fell pack during the 1930s. Whisk quickly engaged and worried his fox, an old male.

Whisk was in action again on **September 25th** after several foxes were up and about before hounds, with a few actually getting to ground. It may be that not many terriers were out that day as only one was accounted for. Whisk killed his fox below after it refused to bolt.

J. Bell was losing hens to foxes in late **October** so on the **28th** the meet was changed from Melbreak to Low Fell and hounds found almost immediately near Latterhead. Reynard gave them a good hunt onto and round Dodd and back to Low Fell where he went to ground and was worried by the terriers.

November 18th was a very misty morning and hounds met at Lanthwaite (pronounced 'Lanthert'). They put a fox off in the bottom of Red Ghyll and then made out for the tops, where hounds ran all day in dense mist, their glorious chorus resounding from the craggy high places announcing their progress, though they were never in view. Charlie succeeded in keeping his brush that day but Ranter, a good young hound, was killed when he fell from Hobcarton Crag.

December 11th was another bad day for the Melbreak as Chancellor and Matchless went down with poison, though Willie doesn't state whether or not they survived. However, whenever Willie used such a term it usually signified death.

It was on **January 13th** that hounds met at Lanthwaite Green and a fox was soon found at Rannerdale Knott, which then gave hounds a fast hunt round Whiteless, Grasmoor and Lad Hows. Charlie then made for Coledale and over to Braithwaite side. Albert wasn't far behind the hounds, having used the high tops to keep in touch, and a weary fox was viewed at Little Braithwaite.

Hounds were a little behind and so Albert unleashed Whisk and off ran the terrier, catching his fox just before hounds arrived and finished off the job.

February 3ʳᵈ witnessed two foxes being roused on Dodd, with one giving a fast hunt to Brandlingill where it went to ground inside a drain. Whisk was once again in action and he quickly worried his quarry. The other fox eventually escaped after giving a good account of itself.

February 6ᵗʰ saw hounds in the Cockermouth district once again where a fox was run to ground at Slate Fell. Mick and Nan (full name Nance) were loosed from their couples and entered the lair, where they soon found. Charlie refused to bolt however and was worried inside the earth.

February 10ᵗʰ witnessed hounds meeting in the Gilgarran district and they found at Winscales Wood and enjoyed a fast hunt round Gilgarran, Jackie Planting and back to Winscales where they ran their fox to earth. Whisk was loosed and he worried a stubborn fox that wouldn't bolt.

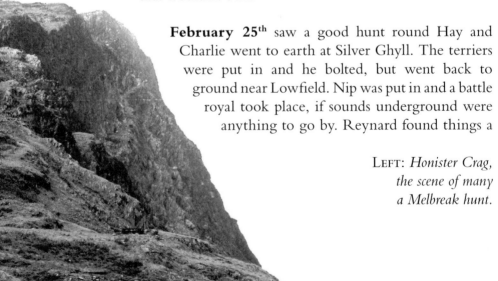

February 25ᵗʰ saw a good hunt round Hay and Charlie went to earth at Silver Ghyll. The terriers were put in and he bolted, but went back to ground near Lowfield. Nip was put in and a battle royal took place, if sounds underground were anything to go by. Reynard found things a

LEFT: *Honister Crag, the scene of many a Melbreak hunt.*

little too hot to handle below ground and eventually bolted from the game terrier, but was pulled down by hounds shortly afterwards.

March 28th was the Quarrymen's Hunt (originally started by the owners of the quarry and was probably hosted by them) and they had a good day, killing one at Hassness and a second at Lower Gatesgarth.

April 6th witnessed a Whinlatter meet and they enjoyed a good hunt round Grisedale Pike and Birkrigg Yaks and then out to Scaw Crags where their fox went to ground at a vast rocky spot. Whisk and Nip were put in with difficulty and they pinned down their quarry and then duly worried it, as it would not bolt and face the hounds again. Nip may have belonged to Jack Pepper, the father of Frank, with whom Willie did much breeding of terriers. If so, this dog was out of Pepper's Pip and Kitchen's famous Central Midge and was obviously a stud fee puppy given back to Jack.

Pepper lived at the now uninhabited Bowder Stone cottage and was a keen follower of both the Melbreak and Blencathra Foxhounds, hunting with each pack as often as possible and supplying both packs with terriers. Frank, Jack's son, worked at Honister Crag as a Quarryman and Jack may well have been employed there too, but I have been unable to discover exactly what Jack did for a living. There were several quarries near his home in the Borrowdale Valley such as at Castle Crag and he may have worked here. The other possibility is that he first moved to this cottage as a guide for tourists, as this was why the homestead was first built in such an isolated location.

The Bowder Stone cottage was built by Joseph Pocklington to house an old woman who acted as a guide to visiting tourists. Both Jack and Frank were serious breeders of the new improved strains of Lakeland terrier and they contributed greatly to both pedigree and unregistered stock.

April 10th was the traditional Good Friday meet when the famous Crummock Water photograph was likely to have been taken. This proved to be a very dry day and scent was extremely difficult. They found at Gate Gills and had a decent hunt, despite the conditions, round the huge bulk of Robinson, which towers above Buttermere, and on to Step Ghyll. Scent gave out about here though and so the hunt failed. After that it was a long tramp back to kennels and the photo was taken as Willie headed towards Lorton Vale at the close of a long day.

Hounds hunted on many occasions during the first half of May and spent at least one week at Buttermere in an attempt to catch up with lamb-worrying foxes. A few were caught and one of the best days was when the hound Royal hunted and killed a fox unaided and alone at Gatesgarth. Call-outs seemed to end about the middle of May and they finished the season with a very respectable fifty-two foxes accounted for. Much of the land was keepered in those days and several foxes were shot, so under the circumstances the hunt had accounted for a large proportion.

ABOVE: *Arthur Irving: shepherd, huntsman and keen terrier breeder.*
RIGHT: *Willie Irving in winning ways with Trim and Mick at Patterdale.*

CHAPTER 8

The Quarrymen's Hunt

The Melbreak traditionally held a quarrymen's hunt in early spring of each year and the meet was always in the Honister district where most of the workers found employment. Yewcrags, Honister and Dubs Quarries have been in use for centuries and hunting has featured largely in the recreation of the workforce at each site. Honister is a fearsome spot formed from volcanic rock which has over time been covered in water and compressed to form the beautiful green slate that has been hacked out of that mountain for generations. This coloured slate protrudes from the ground in places out on the fells, which is how the rich deposits were first discovered.

Mining and quarrying slate was incredibly primitive when it first began and the dates of these first extractions are lost in the mists of time. It is known that the Romans used slate for roofing dwellings associated with Hadrian's Wall and the Vikings may also have made use of this natural material, though it is thought that the Normans may have been the first to bring more advanced mining skills to the British Isles. Or maybe it was the monks who first took advantage of such productive sites as there is much evidence to suggest that they too used slate to roof their large buildings. Whoever first discovered slate around Honister had a nightmare task in extracting it and it seems the first efforts were made above ground, at those sites where rocks made up of slate jutted out of the springy green grass of the fells, or among the wooded slopes.

The poet William Wordsworth describes men in the early 1800s working from wicker baskets suspended from the top of the crag faces by strong ropes. This primitive form of quarrying may well have been in existence from the 13th century onwards, when quarrying in this area had certainly become well established. Production fluctuated throughout the middle-ages, but work was once again giving much employment to folk of the area by the seventeenth century. Underground extraction was well established by the 1700s, but still men hung in wicker baskets well into the 1850s and this way of getting at the rock must have been incredibly dangerous, especially if a sudden storm broke, which is pretty typical of Lake District weather patterns.

This area has some of the worst weather in the British Isles and strong winds and heavy downpours can hit the crags without warning. Local storms bring water cascading down the crags, often dislodging rocks from above. Such rocks hitting one of these wicker baskets would destroy it and the inhabitant would go plunging into the valley below to certain death. Freak winds at Honister were also known as 'wind in the crack' and these sudden blasts were not only deafening, but also life-threatening and legends tell of men being blown off the crag during such storms. Quarrying must have been a nightmare existence, yet it seems to have been a way of life that was loved by many.

Before transport was laid on, the workers would travel to Honister from such far away places as Frizington, Workington, Cockermouth and Keswick, as well as locations in the heart of the Lake District valleys, and stay there during the working week in small bothies built high on the fell, close to the working sites, bringing their own food and other provisions with them. They would then go home for the weekend and return on Monday morning, or even travel back to work during Sunday afternoon. It was a hard existence and some of the workers eventually began living on site permanently.

Their working days were busy enough, but evenings and weekends must have been rather boring and so different forms of recreation sprang from these small mining communities. Music and entertainment, cockfighting, rabbit coursing and hare and fox hunting were popular forms of 'relaxation' for the quarrymen and cock fights actually took place within the mines themselves. Cockfighting in the Lake District, although rightfully outlawed these days, was different from other locations as no artificial spurs were used. Only the natural spurs could be employed and so most of these fights were not to the death and serious injury was often avoided. These men took pride in their birds and would need them, not only for fighting, but in order to keep their hens breeding, so deaths were not welcome, even if the cock had lost its fight.

Sometimes foxes got in among their hens and fighting cockerels, and so hounds would be called in to hunt them down and this may well have been how the Quarrymen's Hunt first got started. Or it may have been that the employers wished to keep their workforce happy and thus organised such activities for them. The Blencathra traditionally hunted the Borrowdale side of Honister, while the Melbreak hunted the Buttermere side. And so hounds were often in the area, though packs would undoubtedly cover this district long before the Blencathra and Melbreak were in existence. My opinion is that a few hounds and terriers would have been kept on site by workers and an old print actually shows one of the quarry workers with a leggy terrier by his side. Hares, foxes, wildcats, otters, pine martens and polecats would all have been hunted using these 'scratch' packs and no doubt a few extra pennies were earned when claiming the bounty given on predators even as late as the 19th century.

Tommy Dobson began hunting his famous Eskdale pack because these funds were available from the bounty system and he began with two great working hounds, Cruiser and Charmer, in 1857, getting ten shillings for every fox brush he handed in and lower fees for other species such as badgers, otters and polecats. Payments were stopped in the Eskdale country in 1883 and so a meeting was held at the King of Prussia Inn, Eskdale (now the King George), with the result that the pack became funded by subscription fees and committees were set up to deal with extra fund-raising. It was the ending of the bounty payments scheme that helped mould the fell packs of the more modern era; and the ending of such payments also brought about the disbanding of several of the smaller packs scattered throughout the county, which could no longer be financed. This also had an effect on fox and badger populations in particular. The bounty payments had meant that several folk hunted down predators, fox and badger being chief among them, for the extra cash this brought. The end of such payments meant predator populations recovered very slowly, but

An early photo of the Melbreak with Richard Head as Huntsman.

gamekeepers still took a heavy toll, and by the mid-twentieth century predator numbers were very healthy indeed, almost too high in fact, as lamb-worrying and poultry killings increased.

1936/37 SEASON

Willie began work on **September 12th** and it was his custom to give hounds a couple of days running foxes (informally hunting to get fit) just to get rid of that excess fat that had been built up over the summer months when hounds were no doubt given a soft life by their walkers.

The first of the fixtures was **September 15th** and a good day was had for so early in the season. There had been a lot of poultry-worrying at, among others, Graythwaite Farm, so Irving took his hounds there in order to deal with the problem. Hounds found right away at Fangs Moss and Reynard quickly went to ground after a short run round the farm, in the old dyke at Bramley Slate. Terriers Rock and Nan were loosed and eagerly entered the dark lair. They quickly found and Charlie wouldn't bolt, so digging commenced and the operation went smoothly. They reached terriers and fox in a relatively short time, but already Rock and Nan had dealt with the hen-worrying problem and the fox was dead. It was thought he was fat with poultry as he seemed unable to give a good run. Another two foxes were roused nearby and one went to earth, being worried by the terriers underground, while foxhounds Singwell and Cracker hunted and killed the other. To Irving's relief, Cracker had obviously been found after he had gone missing for several days close to the west coast.

September 21st saw hounds drawing Carling Knott above Loweswater and several foxes were roused. Hounds settled on just one, which was rather unusual, and it took them round the fell and through the big woods, climbing out to Burnbank and on to Black Crag. They went out by Plough Ghyll now and it was here that Charlie ran to ground, into a rock earth. Terrier Mist was entered and she quickly worried what proved to be a young dog fox when they dug it out. The terrier Mick had featured earlier that day and Mist is mentioned here which leads me to believe this pair might well have been Mockerkin Mike and Mockerkin Mist, two famous Lakeland terriers owned by Tom Meagean. George Henry Long told the author Plummer that several Oregill and Mockerkin dogs served at the Melbreak as it was the aim of the Lakeland Terrier Association to promote working qualities. Many were entered with the pack *after* they had become show champions for fear of them getting 'knocked' for bearing scars and several were loaned to the fell packs for a time, in order to get them going. It was K.C. judges that took a dislike to scars and teeth lost in battle, for LTA judges were usually from a working terrier background and they viewed such marks as badges of honour.

October 2nd witnessed several foxes on the go at Jackie Planting and they enjoyed what Willie termed as "plenty of good hunts." One fox holed under the railway near the Raise, Rock and Nan were sent in to deal with it, as this was in the area where much poultry had been lost to foxes. This pair of extremely game earth dogs quickly set about worrying their fox below ground. **October 9th** was a day spent in the Cockermouth area and scent proved to be incredibly difficult.

However, a badger was found in one of the earths and Willie dug it out at Silver Ghyll.

On **October 27th** a fox gave hounds a good run in the Wythop area, but it met with rather an unusual end. A tourist was motoring in the district and Charlie was unfortunate enough to be in the wrong place at the wrong time and was run over and killed. The hunt committee presented the driver with the mask of this fox, as a reminder of his visit to the area.

It was **November 1st–4th** of this year that Willie and his hounds appeared on stage in a theatre at Cockermouth, with proceeds going to the local hospital. Amateur players put on a show and all nights were a sell-out with hundreds having to be turned away.

Friday **November 27th** was a Shepherd's Meet. This was traditionally when stray sheep were brought along and reunited with their proper owners. A hunt then always took place and there were also other side-events such as stick and terrier shows. And, afterwards, there would usually be a singsong and much eating and drinking! The pack drew from Gate Gills to Robinson and finally had a fox afoot, with Reynard running to Littleton where he went to ground at a rock spot by the side of a steep gryke (crack) in the crag face. Whisk was put in and he duly worried his foe, but became trapped in the process. Meanwhile Irving had drawn for another fox and they soon found, with this one taking hounds to the Honister district where it gave them a grand hunt about the incredibly dangerous Bull Ghyll, the scene of much mining activity. Charlie eventually left this craggy stronghold as hounds pushed him hard from bink to bink and he went out over the high tops above Borrowdale and down to the Newlands Valley where he was lost late on in the day.

   Meanwhile digging operations had commenced back at the earth and on Willie's return it was decided to leave Whisk in overnight. It was a difficult and precarious place to work and they were not going to take any chances during the hours of darkness. Willie, Albert, R. Bewley and Bob Gibson were there at first light on Saturday and they worked all day in horrendous conditions, making slow inroads into the rocky lair while the rain poured from above. A torrent came down the gryke and over the craggy face above, sometimes washing loose rocks down, and the wind howled. But the workers didn't give up and they eventually reached Whisk and his long-dead foe by late afternoon on Sunday, after shifting heavy loads of rock in a hostile environment that could have claimed one or more lives at any time. These fell hunters would literally attempt to shift mountains to get to a trapped terrier.

Hounds drew Carling Knott on **December 4th** amid very cold winter conditions and two foxes were put off. One made round Blake Fell for Burnbank where it went to ground and was worried by Whisk (obviously quickly recovered from his 3-day ordeal) and Nip, while the other made round by Banks, back through Holme Wood to Burnbank and then crossed by Waterend. Charlie finally ran hounds off at Low Fell End. Nip and Whisk were both dog terriers and this adds more testimony that early pedigree Lakelands were not in the least quarrelsome, but were as even-natured as their unregistered counterparts.

January 13th witnessed a meet at Cockermouth Castle and a good hunt was enjoyed round Hay, with Reynard running to earth inside a rabbit warren and Rock and Tess quickly followed, worrying their fox after it refused to bolt. Tess was the dam of Jim Fleming's famous Myrt. Another fox made a good hunt round Higham End and was eventually caught on the road near Higham mansion. The next day saw hounds having a good hunt round the golf links and over Hay, then taking hounds to the Derwent River where it went to earth in a drain at Lowfield. Whisk was again in action, but Charlie refused to bolt and so was duly worried below ground.

February 4th was a superb day in the Cockermouth district and hounds were feathering about in deep heather above Prospect. Charlie could be seen at times as he evaded hounds amongst the deep herbage, but some of the pack leapt into the air and caught glimpses of him as he made through the dark heather tunnels in a wily effort to keep out of their reach. He was at last spied away and hounds almost coursed him out to the top of Lawson Planting, forcing him to go to ground inside a large rabbit hole. Whisk was once again called on to bolt the fox, but few seemed to get away from this gallant earth dog who quickly found and worried an old dog fox, which was dug out soon after. Willie tried for another and drew a lot of ground that day, but, unusually for this area, no other foxes were encountered.

Hounds enjoyed a good day on **March 17th** in the Lamplugh District after a fox was found at Sharp Knott, giving them a run right over the summit of Blake Fell to Ousen Fell, covering much country. He passed Lamplugh Hall and went over the bleak and wild expanse of Howes to Cogra.

He returned to Blake Fell again after passing the reservoir and finally went to ground after dodging hounds at Sharp Knott near to Cogra Moss. Minnie was entered and the bitch terrier quickly worried a fine vixen that was recovered after much digging.

March 19th was another good day and one fox was killed at Kirkstile Wood after giving hounds a run from near Red How. A second was put off by the pack, and this fox took them across the fells to Burnbank and away to cross the head of Loweswater in the low country. Charlie finally made Low Fell and he went to earth at Durling Screes where Tess was entered shortly afterwards. The game little bitch got stuck into her fox and persuaded it to bolt, but it was soon rolled over by hounds.

A meet was held at the kennels on **April 5th** where Mrs Irving laid on generous hospitality, despite now having two young children to take care of. Hounds gave a good hunt for followers round Whiteside and Grasmoor and Charlie finally holed above Hollins.

Terrier Whisk was called in and the fox bolted rather swiftly, but didn't get far as he was caught in the yard of Millar Place less than twenty yards from the kennels. The old vixen was picked up by Mrs Irving, a keen supporter of her husband's pack. It was a memorable day; possibly the only occasion when a fox was accounted for at the kennels themselves.

April 12th, however, stands out for another reason: Chancellor was run over at Lorton Vale and was badly injured. He was taken back to kennels and treated, but it was touch-and-go whether or not he would survive the ordeal.

April 15th witnessed a fine fox being roused near Westray Farm and they had a fast hunt to Cass How Woods where it ran to earth with hounds close on its brush. The heroic little Whisk was put in and he set about finding his quarry, which was lurking somewhere among the rockpiles. Passages led all over this noted stronghold, but Whisk had much experience and Reynard couldn't evade him for long. The game terrier pinned down a fine dog fox and duly worried it before finally being dug out by Jack Ullock and a couple more followers.

A fox was run to ground on **April 19th** after it had given a good run from Armaside. A Mr J. Tinnion (a hunt follower) viewed it away from low-lying fields and a fast hunt ensued. After climbing out of the low country, hounds were taken the whole length of the Wythop fells as far as Lords Seat and then through Aiken Bottoms for Whinlatter. The fox then swung right-handed across Darling How, Sunny Brows and on to Harrot, where Charlie made to earth. Terriers Mist and Nan were then put in and they quickly worried their fox below.

April 23rd saw hounds drawing at Red How Wood, but it was blank. They found at Low Fell however and this fox took them all the way round Melbreak Fell and was finally killed in Crummock Lake at the foot of Park Beck. They roused a second from Lanthwaite Woods and this gave hounds a good hunt on Whiteside before finally going to ground at a rock den and Mac was put in.

Mac was the sire of Felix and would be getting on by this time, but he was still a very useful terrier and was owned by Peter Long who bred early pedigree stock. Mac succeeded in bolting his fox, and hounds soon had it as it made across the fellside. Singwell and

Danger got away on another fox that same day and killed it as a duo at Gatesgarth.

It was while hunting for lamb-worrying foxes in the Buttermere area during **mid-May** that Royal killed a fox after hunting it single-handed from a ledge where four foxes got up at Blea Crags. The pace was excellent and Reynard took the single hound through Blea Combe and to Dodd, eventually making for Burtness. Charlie eventually headed down into the low country and for Raven Crag, where he turned to face the hound, ready to fight, maybe confident that he could see it off. Royal, confused by the action of the fox, halted abruptly, not knowing what to do in such an unusual situation. However, Bob Gibson was nearby with Irving's terrier Nan, who when loosed pitched into its fox without hesitation and shifted it once more. Royal then joined in and the pair finally caught up with Charlie and he was accounted for just behind Gatesgarth Cottage.

Hounds had a few days hunting after lamb-worrying foxes that springtime and they accounted for a few, finishing the season with forty-nine adult foxes killed. There had been much terrier work that season which Whisk, Rock and Nan seemed to feature quite prominently, though, of course, several other terriers also found employment at the hunt.

As the decades passed by the methods employed to mine and quarry the slate improved greatly. More advanced techniques were taught during the nineteenth century by experts from Wales who had perfected slate quarrying back in their native country. These new Welsh methods were adopted at both Coniston and Honister and it is my belief that these miners brought Welsh terriers with them to the Lake District and that these then entered into local terrier strains. Irving, in one of his many letters, stated that Jack Pepper's strain of Bowder Stone Lakeland terrier was rather Welsh in type and many produced good quality black and tan stock. The Coniston hunt also produced good quality black and tan terriers and I am certain much of their ancestry was due to Welsh terriers entering local strains from the 1850s. Working ability would not have suffered from such 'alien' blood: these Welsh strains of terriers were also used to control foxes in a similar landscape and were very familiar with large rocky earths. Many have wondered where the good quality black and tan of the Coniston terriers and of Pepper's strain arose, and I believe such questions have now been answered.

The miners at Honister included many characters and some became very good entertainers and musicians, while others became involved in far less respectable pursuits. A chap called Moses Rigg lived and worked at Dubs Quarry, but his main source of income was smuggling good quality French brandy and distilling whisky. Exactly where he distilled this fiery brew is impossible to say, but it was somewhere within the vicinity of Honister and Dubs Quarries and may have been in the mines themselves, or hidden at some spot out on the fells in much the same way as the Irish distilled their potato water. Wherever and however Rigg conducted his highly illegal operation there was no shortage of customers for his incredibly strong drink and it is said that when he was finally caught he got off with a light sentence, avoiding going to prison, because many of the legal profession and gentry regularly purchased brandy and whisky indirectly from him. 'Laal' Lanty Lee was another Lake District character who was engaged in much the same activity as Rigg.

Life was incredibly hard at Honister and it is said that, in such an isolated spot, much of their food would be going off by the end of the week, yet they had no choice but to eat it, or starve. They worked from early morning until well into the evening, but were allowed weekends off, which gave them a chance to be with their families and engage in their interests, such as hunting. It was mostly quarrymen and miners who kept the terriers, together with one or two hounds, and they brought these together on Saturday or Sunday and enjoyed long and tiring hunts with their bobbery packs. Wildcats (when they still existed in the Lake District), otters, foxes, deer, badgers, polecats, pine martens, rats and rabbits were all hunted with these packs and they produced outstanding working dogs who made up much of the backbone of Lakeland terrier stock when the name was adopted in 1912. Many of these terriers were also on loan to the many different packs of hounds in those days and there were far more of these packs before the First World War, than in modern times. There were many official packs, true, but there were also several private packs of hounds, as well as bobbery packs, and much work was enjoyed by these terriers of old, which helped shape an incredibly game and unique type of earth dog.

Pack ponies were used to carry the quarried slate away from the almost sheer-drop slopes of Honister and the waste was simply tipped over the edge where it cascaded down the mountainside to form huge screes which are clearly seen today.

Such screes were difficult for hounds to cross when in pursuit of their fox; impossible to negotiate for hunt staff and followers intent on keeping with the pack. The pack horse routes were often very difficult to negotiate and one of the worst was known as Moses Trod, possibly because the smuggler Moses Rigg had used the route to bring in his illegal goods from Ravenglass, or some hidden cove nearby. This route led for miles over to Wasdale Head and from here slate was taken to the port of Ravenglass where it would then go on to fulfil orders from customers.

One of the ways in which slate was transported away from the mine itself was by the use of 'sledging'. These were large wooden baskets or barrows filled with slate and then dragged away by a chap holding onto the two front spars. These men then led the sledge down the steep fellside, very often traversing Bull Ghyll, and steered over the screes to the road below.

This was a job for young and fit men and the technique was hair-raising. No doubt injuries were common among those learning how to carry out this skilful procedure, though once perfected, several loads could be successfully taken down the mountain during the course of a typical working day and no doubt competition and wagers were common among this sporting breed of people.

Willie started work on **September 13th** and they had some very productive hunting once the fixtures began from **September 20th**.

October 4th was a particularly good day and the pack drew Melbreak Fell, finding several foxes at Mowdy Crags. They enjoyed a good hunt and finally holed a couple of foxes at the top of the crags. Whisk and Nip, both heroes of the previous season, were put to ground and they worried one fox and bolted another, which gave hounds a good run before going to earth once again, near Crummock Lake. Charlie bolted a second time once the terrier had got at him, but this time he didn't get far and was pulled down in the lake itself.

October 11th was a Rigg House meet and several foxes were roused, but scent was poor indeed. Six hounds got away on one fox and ran

Maud with Albert Thomas in the summer of 1931. Albert remained a close family friend after he left the Melbreak.

it to Bowness Knott above Ennerdale Water where it headed below ground in an attempt to keep its brush. Albert Thomas managed to follow them and he had Whisk and Nip by his side, who he loosed into the earth. He then dug out a vixen that had been worried by this game pair.

October 12th saw them at the same place yet again and they failed to find until they reached the wild and windy Winscales. They had a fox stirring soon after and hunted it to Wythmoor Pit Wood where Reynard sought sanctuary below ground. Whisk was once more called upon to oblige and this he did with his usual gusto, worrying a fine dog fox, which was eventually dug out.

Hounds had several foxes going once again on **October 29th** and they enjoyed a few good hunts, with one fox being lost about Swinside after hounds had pushed it hard. A Mr Coates went to feed his hens later in the day and to his astonishment a fox bolted from inside the hen house where it had earlier hidden from the relentless pack.

The gallant pack met at Lamplugh Green on **January 14th** and they found at Carling Knott after drawing for some distance without success. They then had a very fast hunt through Holme Wood, the wonderful music swelling among the cluster of trees clinging to the steep fellside, and away to Burnbank. They crossed Fangs and on by Ask Hill Knott to Watering Wood where their fast fleeing quarry holed and stood its ground when terriers Nan and Nip were entered. This brace of game earth dogs worried their fox below ground after a terrific struggle. When Willie returned to kennels, or maybe at the pub that night, he got word that a carcass of a fox had been found and they were certain it was that of a fox they thought had been accounted for near Thornthwaite village on **October 16th**. Quite a number of hunts ended without a result being known and a fox carcass would be found sometime later that would bring about a satisfactory conclusion. Shepherds and quarrymen, or hunt followers wandering among isolated places often found such carcasses.

January 31st saw hounds at Gilgarran on a very wild and stormy day. The pack found at Friar Bank and had a short and fast spin to the railway where Reynard went to ground. Jerry and Nip were put in and they quickly set about finishing a fine dog fox that was dug out after much effort.

They were at the Castle on **February 11th** and soon found in the forestry. They then had a good hunt round Hay and Charlie went to earth at Andrew Bank and was duly finished below ground after terriers Jerry and Pinch had been entered there.

February 18th witnessed a meet at Scale Bridge and they enjoyed a grand hunt round Dodd and back down by Scale. The pack crossed at Bowderbeck and went out round Moss, then in down Sandy Combe Edge. The fox took them back by Wood House, Lake Head and back to Scale where it finally made to ground. Pinch, Nip and Nan were put in and the fox was very quickly dug out and saved from the terriers, which had struggled to get in this tight and narrow place, otherwise Charlie would have been dead for certain. He was set on his feet again, but hounds overtook him soon after and accounted for a fine dog fox.

On **March 23rd** hounds had a fast hunt from Thunder Ghyll and the fox holed at Burtness Combe. Nip and Nan followed their fox into its rock den, but it would not bolt and so was worried underground.

April 1st saw hounds marking an earth at Watering Wood and Tinker and Tess, the sire and dam of Fleming's Myrt, were loosed and entered. They soon found their skulking quarry but it refused to bolt, so was dug out in short time and set on its feet. Hounds caught it some time later on the Mosser road. Hounds then enjoyed a fast hunt on a second fox and killed it about the bottom of Fellbarrow. A third fox was soon afoot and gave a good hunt round Melbreak, but was lost late in the day near Kirkstile.

Friday **April 29th** was the day of a meet at Croasdale, at Spedding's farm no doubt, and they had a fox running at Scaw, which went to earth in Cleaves Ghyll, at a difficult spot. W. Gibson's Nip was put in and somehow became trapped below ground. The fox wouldn't bolt and so Willie drew on for another that took them to Rannerdale Knott where it was lost, but he returned to the earth later and helped with the rescue. This epic rescue continued until the following Monday, when Nip was recovered after much digging and effort. Pepper's Nip and W. Gibson's Nip both served at the Melbreak and it is difficult to know which of the two is in use at any given time, unless Willie states it, though by this date it is logical to reason that Pepper's Nip would probably have been retired.

May 10th was the last hunting day of the season and scent was impossible as Willie records they had had "no rain for over a month." They finished with a very respectable seventy-two foxes being accounted for in total, and the high numbers taken were reflected in fewer lambing troubles that springtime, though they were called out on a few occasions.

Quarrymen didn't just enjoy hunting during the Quarrymen's Hunt at springtime, but would engage in this activity at every opportunity and they would often down tools to assist Willie, or previous Huntsmen, whenever hounds were in the area. One such memorable occasion was November 23rd 1937 after hounds had met at Gate Gills. They found at Gatesgarth and had a fast hunt up the dale where one can now traverse the Honister Pass, in the shadow of the mighty fells and huge jutting crags that loom menacingly over this area.

  Charlie made for Honister Quarries and hounds soon followed, capturing the attention of workers who were carrying out different tasks out in the open, some among the crags themselves, the music of the pack echoing wildly amongst the rock faces all over this district, their glorious music rebounding from place to place. And when

Charlie 'binked' at Drum House crag, Willie needed the assistance of the quarrymen. This is a fearsome spot for hounds and terriers are not often loosed to shift a fox from a ledge in such dangerous surroundings, so the kindly chaps at Honister gladly helped out and stoned the fox out of the crag. Reynard then gave hounds a fine hunt to Buxom Hows and decided to go to earth there. Terriers were put in, but the fox wouldn't bolt and so digging operations began. Charlie was worried before he could be reached and an old dog fox was finally uncovered after much hard graft. That cunning fox had climbed like a cat to an impossible place among the crags and neither hound nor terrier could hope to follow, so he would have escaped for sure had not the quarrymen obliged and shifted the fox off its ledge.

1938/39 SEASON

Willie began hunting on **September 19th** and the day proved sunny and warm with few foxes about. However, they soon had one going and enjoyed a good hunt, despite the unfavourable conditions, with a fox that took hounds twice round the huge bulk of Melbreak Fell. Charlie then went to ground above Green Wood and Nip followed as soon as Willie had reached the spot where his eager pack marked. The terrier bolted his fox soon after and it was killed on the fell breast after a short run. Not a bad start to the season at all!

The opening meet on **October 6th** was a wild and windy day, but at least the rain held off. Several foxes were astir at Watering Wood and most of the pack got onto the line of one which took them out of woodland and away to Low Fell where they effected a kill down by the fell fence above Oak Bank. A few hounds got away on a second fox from the woodland and this took them to Durling where it crept below, with hounds close behind. Charlie was then bolted by the terriers, but he went to earth again as hounds pushed him hard. He was bolted and holed repeatedly before finally being accounted for above Mosser Road End. A busy day for the terriers.

October 29th proved a glorious day in the Buttermere area and hounds met at Low bank. The lake mirrored the rich, vivid autumn colours and even locals, who saw these sights regularly, were compelled to 'stand and stare', taking in the wondrous views all around. A slowish hunt began about Lad Hows (pronounced 'Laddas') and along by Whiteless to Wandope Crags where the quarry went to ground among the rocks. Nigger was unshackled and he entered the earth eagerly, searching out his foe among the dark piles of rock and finding it skulking in a dark and narrow passage, from where it lunged at the game terrier. Nigger wasn't in the least intimidated and he seized his quarry, which then dragged him out of the earth and into full view of hounds, hunt staff and followers. Running off with Nigger's jaws attached to him, the weight of the terrier slowed this game and gallant fox and hounds quickly had him. He was a fine dog fox of over seventeen pounds in weight and he was the fifteenth secured fox of the season so far.

December 15th witnessed hounds meeting at Darling How and they found at Aiken Plantation, with a fast hunt ensuing. Reynard took them to Whinlatter, Darling How, Wythop Fells and on through Wythop to Hundith Hill where they caught and killed him on the drive of what is now the Hundith Hill Hotel. This residence was in those days a private country house. Willie took a number of foxes from this area over the years and many hunts passed through the grounds of Hundith Hill.

LEFT: *Maud Irving with a young hound.*
RIGHT: *Hound and terrier breeding often took place during the close season of the summer. Young Maud with hound and terrier puppies.*

The pack met at the Star Inn on **April 10th** and a fox was quickly afoot at Jackie Planting, which gave a good run round by Gilgarran and then back to Jackie, where its brush was claimed. A fine dog fox was accounted for. Lambs had been being taken from White Keld farm and a vixen and cubs were found in a lair at Jackie Planting and dug out. The vixen was indeed the culprit as remains were found at her chosen den.

May 6th was the last lambing call of that season, but it was a very bad scenting day, being far too warm and dry and so there were no signs of game. The Melbreak finished that last season before the outbreak of World War II with sixty-four foxes accounted for and this was a good tally, for they had lost many days to bad weather as snow and severe frost had been a feature of that winter, as well as dry and impossible scenting conditions.

Much of the work at Honister was labour-intensive and the low population of the Lakes country meant that such labour was often hard to come by, so outside workers were often brought in. As we have

already seen, quite a number of Welsh miners worked at Coniston Old Man and Honister mines, teaching more advanced extraction methods, and Irish labour was also brought in, particularly during the nineteenth century when large groups of 'navvies' worked out the rock and cleared ways for tramlines etc. Just as the Welsh brought their game little tykes with them, so did the Irish.

The Irish terrier certainly went into the mix that was to produce what would later become known as the Lakeland terrier. Irish settlers have arrived on Cumbrian shores for at least the last three centuries and seasonal farm workers also brought many into the area, so it is not surprising that Irish terrier bloodlines played an important role in the development of 'coloured working terriers' as fell and Lakeland terriers were once known.

I am certain that the harsh coated earth dog known as the Patterdale terrier was descended from fell stock infused with Irish and Welsh bloodlines that moved the breed away from the Bedlington type. These differed from the Bedlington-blooded fell terriers in that they had good quality coats, powerful heads and narrower shoulders. It was the old Patterdale terrier that became known as the Lakeland after 1912. The Melbreak, even during the nineteenth century, was well known for producing red, hard-coated terriers – proof of Irish terrier influence.

Barracks were built to house the workers and they included recreation rooms where the men could socialise during the week. It was never intended that anyone should actually live on site, but several did, refusing to go home at weekends and ending up living on site permanently, except for trips into Keswick where wild drinking sessions were the norm. The Irish workers had a lively approach to leisure-time and the more reserved Cumbrians had a tough time accepting them for a while, with the two communities being kept separate for some time. Many of these Irish moved on when the workload lessened at Honister, but many also remained in the north and several Cumbrian families are descended from these settlers. They may have been wild, these Irish grafters, but they enjoyed their sport and added to the enthusiasm for game terriers and hard-hunting hounds. In fact, the Irish are noted for their passion for hound work and in the absence of such, even street curs would be employed to hunt almost anything that moved. Bobbery packs were common in Ireland, and the west of Cumbria in particular had a tradition that would match that back in Eire.

As quarrying and mining at Honister became more and more efficient, better ways of transporting the finished product were employed, such as carts pushed along tramlines. The tramway became known as 'the Monkey Shelf' and was a much better and safer way of shifting tons of rock to the finishing sheds. However, the old method of 'sledging' rock continued for quite some time after tramways were put in, at the upper reaches of the crag in particular and this must have been an amazing spectacle to observe.

Accidents did happen and people were killed at Honister, but one of the worst of all accidents happened in 1965 and this involved Frank 'Pont' Pepper, the son of Jack, and breeder of game Lakeland terriers with the 'Bowder Stone' prefix.

In order to reduce the numbers of those living on site, the management had introduced a bus service that could pick up workers in the morning and drop them near their homes in the evening each day of the working week. One such service ran from Keswick all the way down the Borrowdale Valley and no doubt Frank Pepper took full advantage of this. Frank was working in the Fiddlers closehead (named after two musicians who entertained the workers with music on the fiddle) when he was hit by a fall of rock.

Legend has it that he fell from a ladder at the mine, but that doesn't seem to be the case at all, unless he was up a ladder at the time of the rock fall. Whatever the actual circumstances surrounding the accident, the result was truly horrific. He received head injuries that were bad enough, but the worst injuries were to his back, with several bones being broken. He was taken to Keswick hospital and then transferred to a specialist unit in Sheffield where he would spend many months recovering. His injuries left him unable to walk again and he returned to the fells only to be housed in an adapted cottage at Grange, Borrowdale, where he lived, a shadow of his former self. He was a life-long supporter of the Melbreak and a pal of Irving's, with whom he bred terriers. Willie used a number of the Pepper strain of

Summer work at Cockermouth cemetary. Willie and
'Mowdy' Robinson are sitting on the wall.

Lakeland for both breeding and working back at the Melbreak hunt
and continued to use this strain on his bitches after his retirement.
Frank was a keen terrierman and it must have been heart-rending
for him not to be able to get out on those fells again and work his
extremely useful and typey earth dogs.

Honister closed down in 1986 and became a sad graveyard of a
place where once much activity had been carried out, with its own
community and social structure, of which hunting was an integral

part. For about a decade the only sounds then coming from this place were the mournful winds rattling across the rock-strewn fell tops and howling amongst the tunnels carved out of the crag face by generations of workers. But I am happy to write that Honister is now a working and lively place once again, though it thrives more from tourism these days, than as the working quarry it once was. Mark Weir and his partner bought the quarry lease during the latter half of the 1990s and started workings again. They now produce all kinds of products from this beautiful slate, including worktops and garden ornaments. Tours of the mines are conducted each day and the place is well worth a visit.

Honister is a very atmospheric place and the landscape is awe-inspiring and forbidding to say the least. I talked with one of the quarry workers and he told me of a time when he had stood with Johnny Richardson, the famous Blencathra Huntsman, at Yew Crags, watching hounds work a fox out of Honister crags. Suddenly a hound fell from the narrow ledge and went as stiff as a board as it tumbled down the crags and to the screes below, to certain death. And I wondered how many hounds, terriers, indeed, even people, had met a similar fate at this hostile, yet compelling, place.

1939/40 SEASON

War broke out in September 1939 but Willie, at the age of 41, was too old to be conscripted. In any case he had a reserved occupation as a shepherd and huntsman, being commissioned by the Ministry of Agriculture to use hounds and terriers for the purpose of driven fox shoots.

Willie should have returned to his duties on Tuesday **September 12th** and the first hunt was from the kennels on **September 16th**. He had received a severe ankle injury however, after slipping from a moving tractor and was out of action for a good part of that season. Joe Hind of Buttermere helped out. This was a poor day for scent and hounds couldn't follow any of the several foxes they roused.

October 12ᵗʰ was the opening meet at Kirkstile and Willie loosed hounds at Watering Wood where they had several foxes going. They holed two at Low Fell End and these were worried below by the terriers and a third fox made back for Watering Wood where it too went to earth and was worried underground.

November 17ᵗʰ witnessed hounds meeting at Dean and they found at Outgang from where they enjoyed a fast hunt round by Arlecdon church and back by Tutehill. The pack made good ground from here and caught their fox near the Greyhound Inn, which was a popular meet venue. Another fox was afoot from Jackie Planting and this too gave hounds a fast hunt, finally being accounted for in Loweswater Lake.

November 24ᵗʰ was the Shepherds' Meet at Gate Gill and they failed to find until they reached the formidable Yew Crags and had Reynard afoot out of the rocks. He then gave them a good hunt through Seatoller fell and Gillercombe, then back to Honister Crag where they were forced to leave him. Even the quarrymen couldn't shift him from this stronghold and neither hound nor terrier could hope to follow their more agile opponent.

It seems Albert Thomas had resigned after the 1938/39 season as, when Willie was forced to remain at home laid up with flu in December, Joe Hind was still assisting the Huntsman. Albert had asked for a pay rise, but he was refused and so reluctantly resigned. He remained a keen supporter of the Melbreak, however, as well as a close Irving family friend who continued to keep and breed Willie's strain of Lakeland terrier. Hind took hounds out on **December 19ᵗʰ** and had a good hunt, which ended with Charlie making to earth and being worried there by the terriers.

December 22ⁿᵈ saw Irving back in action and the meet was at Peel Wyke. The pack enjoyed a very good hunt round the woods and they holed their fox near the fell top above Peel Wyke. Smiler, quite a well known pedigree Lakeland that played quite an important role in breeding circles of the late 30s and early 40s, was put in and it seems the fox was drawn, or bolted with the terrier hanging on, as hounds and the terrier finished the job.

There had been a lot of hard frost and heavy snow, with hounds confined to kennels for over a week during late January and early February so **February 5th** was the next hunt of some note. Joe Hind was in charge, as Willie was laid up with illness again, and they had a long hunt from Winscales, which ended when Reynard went to earth in sand holes near Calva. W. Gibson's terrier, Nip, was entered, but was never heard of again. No other terriers were put in and one can only assume that the poor tyke suffocated in the sandy earth, maybe after tackling a badger, or possibly the fox that ran in, though no sounds were heard. W. Gibson was possibly the son of Bob Gibson, the renowned Lakeland terrier breeder and lifelong supporter of the Melbreak Foxhounds.

February 6th was at West-croft and Foxhounds Trixie and Shifty went away on a fox, which they accounted for at Weddicar Parks. A second was run to High Walton, near St Bees, but was lost there. **April 14th** witnessed a meet at Swin-side and they enjoyed a fast hunt from Thwaites Planting and it is thought they killed in the wood

Willie and Maud, with their daughters Maud (junior) and little Pearl (who is holding Rusty).

bottom. Seven hounds had got onto the line of another fox and they went in by Braithwaite and crossed all the way to Skiddaw, Latrigg and away to near Threlkeld village where they finally lost the scent. This was a mammoth hunt of several miles and who knows how far they would have gone had scent held out.

They finished the season on **May 7th** and Joe Hind, it seems, was in charge again. He had a successful hunt and hounds killed in fields below Keskadale after a long run from Buttermere that took in several of the high fells of this wild district. Fifty-nine foxes was the final tally and this was very respectable considering that harsh weather had stopped them for several days.

CHAPTER 9

Summer Occupations

In order to keep running costs down, the hunt committees decided that the appointed Huntsman and Whipper-in should be relieved of duties during the summer when hounds went back to their walks and that they should find alternative employment until it was once again time to gather in hounds and begin fulfilling hunt fixtures. At the end of the season some hounds would go back to walk, but a good number would also be kept in kennel to deal with problem foxes during lambing time. These calls usually ended by about the middle of May and then the rest would go back to walkers, with maybe one or two pregnant bitches being left in kennel, along with a few terriers, though some of the terriers also went back to those who either loaned them to the hunt, or walked them for the hunt. Kennel maintenance would be carried out during the last two weeks of May and then alternative work would have to be found for the more gentle summer months. And so Huntsmen and Whips had to be resourceful as they had to turn their hands to a number of different tasks.

One of the early jobs Willie carried out during the summer was stone chipping. There was a ruined house near Millar Place and he would get stones from this and break them up, the resultant chippings being used as road laying material. His daughter Maud, only a little girl at the time, can remember her father wearing gauze goggles to protect his eyes from the flying splinters of rock. Mowdy Robinson also carried out this work and Irving may have come across this job through him. He found such employment early in his career, but he also worked on farms, particularly at Gatesgarth with Alan Nelson and then, a little later, with the Richardson family. Willie was already an experienced farmer and any tenant would have received good, expert experience from him, whether cattle, sheep, or poultry needed tending. He would be especially useful helping gather in flocks in readiness of shearing, as he was prepared to walk tirelessly on the fells for hours, covering several miles at a stretch. He worked on various farms and was a popular and hardworking farmhand who really knew his trade. Huntsmen have always been popular figures in the Lake District and they had few problems finding employment at the season's end.

1940/41 SEASON

War broke out in late 1939 and Albert Thomas had joined up sometime after this, along with many other Lakelanders, including Joe Wear, the Ullswater Huntsman, who was replaced by Anthony Barker who had to juggle with helping to produce the nation's food and hunting hounds for the sole purpose of fox control amid difficult conditions. Joe Hind had spent a season as Whipper-in, but now it was decided, due to the need to be frugal during wartime, that Willie should hunt hounds single-handed, which was quite a task in those days without vehicles and CBs to help him keep in touch with the pack.

Willie began hunting with seventeen couple on **September 11th** 1940 and they killed at Whiteside. **September 18th** was a bad day in that three hounds were killed at Lanthwaite Woods, though Irving doesn't state how.

The meet was at Lanthwaite Woods on **September 23rd** and a fine fox was found on Grasmoor who took them over Grisedale Pike and to Eel Crags. Reynard stayed among the crags for a while and hounds had great difficulty working him out of this rough place, but he eventually made for more open ground, sticking to boulder-strewn country in an attempt to slow hounds. They persisted and pressed him hard and he eventually went to ground in Long Crags. Terrier Pinch was loosed when Willie arrived and he followed his fox into this deep rocky lair. Charlie wasn't for bolting and tried to fight off the terrier from a good vantage-point, but Pinch was just too game and worried his foe in the dark recesses of the earth. A second fox was soon afoot and this too went to ground at Corn How and was also worried below ground.

October 17th saw hounds meet at Rigg House and they quickly found below Gilgarran. They had a fast hunt to Bannockrow where Charlie holed and was worried by the terriers. A second fox gave hounds a superb run round the Gilgarran district and was holed and bolted five times before being killed. Poor Nigger was dug out of one of these holes after bolting his fox and he was found to be stone dead. Heart failure possibly, or maybe he had suffocated.

October 18th saw a fox roused from Jackie Planting and it was reluctant to leave cover. Hounds forced it away in the end and a fast hunt ensued that took them across Winscales and almost to Harrington, but then the fox turned and made for Barfs Quarry where it went to earth among the piles of rock. Melbreak Dobbie and Meg soon

The old Buttermere Hotel where Willie and his pack often stayed. It is now a Youth Hostel.

Irving and his hounds meet outside the Pheasant Inn at Wythop, Cumbria.

followed and they were heard hard at their fox, which refused to shift. And so digging tools were sent for and operations began, which proved to be difficult, but after much effort the brace of terriers and their now-dead vixen were reached and this brought an end to a good and successful day.

Willie's father died on **December 5th** and so he took hounds home and they didn't hunt again that week.

December 20th was at Rannerdale and Jack Porter was in charge that day and he loosed and had a fox away from Lad Hows, which, after running the high fells, headed down to near Lorton Village and went to ground in Pearson's drain. Albert Thomas was home on leave, having joined up some time earlier, and he had walked out with Willie's terriers. He now put in Nip and Dart, which worried their fox inside the lair. Albert did own one or two of his own terriers, but Nip was Irving-bred and Dart, though bred by Willie, was owned by Joe Armstrong. **March 19th** was a Lamplugh meet and hounds enjoyed a good and exciting hunt in Holme Wood and on away to Burnbank, where the fox sought refuge in a holly tree and was accounted for.

April 18th was a meet from kennels and they had a blank morning, so Willie returned hounds and was putting them away when two hounds, Tulip and Delver, came over Dodd on the line of a fox they had obviously roused after sneaking away from the pack. Willie quickly loosed the rest and they all joined forces, having a grand hunt on the heights of Whiteside and Howes. Charlie then took them down into the low country and back up Hope Ghyll, only to be rolled over behind Hope Farm. The Melbreak had a record season of eighty-three foxes accounted for, despite the fact that Irving was single-handed that season. Also, they had lost many days to bad weather, heavy snow and hard frost in particular, though there were also some wild and stormy days. They hunted almost to the end of May, but did little after the middle of that month.

Willie Irving had grown up with farming and so could earn an income from this trade during the summer, though as mentioned he also took up other employment, such as stone chipping. Another job he took was cutting grass with scythes at Cockermouth cemetery alongside Mowdy Robinson and a few others, which he really enjoyed (see page 144). He became very proficient with a scythe and used one all his life on his own garden. Willie and his wife were keen gardeners and enjoyed growing much of their own fruit and vegetables. However, the exploits of his terriers and the fact that they were reported in the newspapers made them very popular and so he also made quite a bit of money from stud fees and selling puppies, not just to show people, but also to working homes. His stock found a ready market all over England, Wales, Scotland and Ireland and even some southern hunts used his strain of Lakeland terrier with their packs of hounds. His large collection of letters indicate that a great many of his puppies went to working homes and people often came back for more, which tells us something of the quality of his stock.

1941/42 SEASON

The hunting began on **September 10th** and it was thought they killed about Aiken Bottom, the cover being too dense to recover the carcass.

They accounted for an old fox on **October 31st** near Whitbeck Bridge which had been a renowned poultry killer, taking several chickens from Hope Farm. Such experiences demonstrate the value of a pack of hounds carrying out pest control during war time, when every egg was valuable.

The Shepherds' Meet was at the Fish Hotel, Buttermere, on **November 28th** and a grand hunt was enjoyed. The conversation at this meet was usually about farming, but this time the war dominated the chatter. It was quite good weather for the time of year, though there had been severe gales that week. A fox was roused from Knott Rigg and a fast hunt followed that took hounds through Keskadale Yaks and down across the wide and scenic Newlands Valley. Over Mosey Bank they ran and on to Littleton, going up the valley and then climbing out onto the massive bulk of Robinson Fell, which looms menacingly above the small hamlet at Buttermere. Reynard took the oncoming pack all the way to the summit of this grand and majestic fell and then made to earth at an awkward spot in Robinson Crag.

Gypsy of Melbreak, a famous and popular pedigree bitch that was one of the ancestors, among others, of the Oregill strain of Lakeland terrier, was loosed and she crept carefully along the rocks and disappeared below ground. Gypsy was soon heard at her fox and it decided to get out of there rather speedily. Charlie bolted amongst the craggy features of Robinson and made his way out onto a narrow and dangerous ledge. Gypsy emerged soon after and followed her fox onto the crag, but the poor lass lost her footing and fell down the crag face for a considerable distance, with a sickening bump or two along the way. She was badly injured and had to be carried back to kennels and cared for, but, thankfully, she made a full recovery. Reynard had to be left in this most dangerous of places. Gypsy was so popular and had such a good reputation as a worker that her fall put a dampener on spirits for the rest of that day.

December 29th was a Melbreak Fell meet and they had a fast hunt from Mosedale and over to Mowdy Crag where their fox went to ground. Rusty and Meg were put in and the fox bolted some time later with the two terriers hanging onto it and hounds were quickly there, accounting for their quarry. A second fox was killed at Tenters at exactly the same spot as a fox had been killed only the week before.

January 1st was a good day and they found at Beck head Moss. A fast hunt followed to Low Fell and across to Dodd where hounds split. One lot holed the original fox at Birkin End. It bolted from the terrier, but was soon rolled over by Tulip. The other hunt proved a long one and took in a few of the high fells above Lorton Vale and eventually went down into the low country. Reynard headed now for High Lorton and he was killed in the schoolyard.

Hounds marked a badger sett near Mockerkin village on **February 11th** and Meg, alongside another terrier, was entered. A fox bolted, but another was to ground and was worried by the terriers. A hard dig recovered the carcass and it was discovered that Meg had been badly mauled. Hounds hunted the bolted fox by Carling Knott and killed about Mockerkin How.

The Kirkstile Inn at Loweswater: 'home of the Melbreak foxhounds'.

February 24th saw the first of the fox shoots that were necessary now that most hunting folk were away fighting the war. They were in the Cockermouth area and four foxes were shot, while two were accounted for by hounds. Willie always worried about his hounds during these shoots because there was a danger that hounds could be injured or killed by an over–enthusiastic gun.

March 1st was another shooting day at Wythop Hall. Five were shot and one dug out using terriers, while another was killed by two hounds on the road.

March 13th witnessed a meet at Ling Fell and they quickly had a fox afoot, which took them close to Strawberry How where it went to ground. Willie dug the fox and as he was pulling it out of the earth it bit his hand quite badly. Hounds then quickly accounted for it.

On **April 12th** Tulip fell fifty-feet from crags at Robinson Fell whilst working a fox out of there and she was badly knocked about, but made a good recovery.

April 23rd was a Lanthwaite meet and they hit off a drag from the green and eventually holed their fox at Grasmoor Point. Peat (registered with the K.C. as Border Peat) and Meg followed and accounted for a fine vixen that was dug out after much hard work. **May 20th** was the last lambing call and six cubs were dug out at Ask Hill Knott. Sixty-five foxes were accounted for that season and shoots would now become a feature of wartime fell hunting.

CHAPTER 10

Keen Supporters

Jack Moore of Rigg House was one of the keenest of all supporters and a good breeder of quality Lakeland terriers which played a large part in the founding of early strains. His stock worked with the Melbreak under Huntsmen Jonathan Banks and Richard Head, as well as during Irving's time at the hunt. He was a keen and expert farmer too and played a major role in getting Young Farmers clubs organised in West Cumbria. Huntsman, Whip, hounds and terriers were catered for when in this district and Moore was always on hand to help dig out a fox, or a trapped terrier. Jack greatly encouraged the young with regard to farming and hunting and he was a credit to the Melbreak pack, as well as to his own local community. Several of Willie's strain of terrier, along with many others, could be traced back to the earth dogs bred by and belonging to Jack Moore and it seems this sporting farmer also walked hounds and terriers for the pack.

J. Spedding of Croasdale was yet another sporting farmer who walked hounds and terriers for the Melbreak pack and this may well have been the same Spedding who owned a famous ancestor of all pedigree Lakeland terriers called Scamp. If so, then this may well have been the same Scamp that saw much service at the Melbreak during the 1920s and 30s. There was also a Spedding at Egremont and the two may well have been closely related, but which of them owned Scamp remains a mystery. My money would be on Spedding of Croasdale.

Another keen early supporter was a Cockermouth builder and hunter, Jack Allison. He was also known for breeding good terriers and these served at both the Cumberland and Melbreak packs. His nephew was J.W. Allison, a chemist who also supported his local packs and continued the family tradition of breeding useful terriers. Charlie Fisher of Distington Hall was a well-known figure who supported both the Cumberland and Melbreak Foxhounds. Even into his advanced years he remained very fit and active and lived out his later life at Cockermouth.

George Wilkie of Moresby was another good supporter and he was noted at one time for his top winning horse, Joey, which did very well at hunt point-to-point races popular in this part of the world. Hamilton Docherty was another and he had a son of the same name whom Willie grew up with. He and young Hamilton used to play truant from school to follow hounds and were often found assisting the Huntsman of a pack of beagles kennelled at St Bees, or following in the wake of Willie Porter and his Eskdale and Ennerdale pack.

Young Hamilton Docherty was a keen breeder of terriers and used Willie's strain to keep the sheer guts in his own. Although a keen follower of the Melbreak he eventually took up a post as school-teacher at Calderbridge and mainly followed the Eskdale and Enner-dale, which were within easier reach.

Mr and Mrs Greenhow had the Fish Hotel *(see opposite)* and they always provided great hospitality whenever hounds met there. When in this area hounds and hunt staff usually stayed at the Butter-mere Hotel (now the youth hostel), or at Gatesgarth farm, or with the Hind family when called in during lamb-worrying at springtime. Mr and Mrs Stagg tenanted the Kirkstile Inn and they too were famous for their keen hospitality and especially for their 'tattie pot' suppers that were eagerly partaken of after a day out hunting among the high places.

Many a good hunt was from the Kirkstile Inn and this place became known as the home of the Melbreak Foxhounds. Many a celebration was had at this Inn and some of the revellers would fall asleep in one of the outbuildings and spend the night there after being 'overcome' by the sharp and pure mountain air mingling with the large quantities of ale!

1942/43 SEASON

An early start was made on **September 6th** at Whiteside, but they failed to find. They were at Rigg House on **October 30th** and found at Jackie Planting, the hunt taking them to badger holes at Hodyoad Ghyll, Scalesmoor. They dug out two large sow badgers which the terriers had turned their attention to, but Reynard wasn't located.

November 27th was the Shepherds' Meet and they enjoyed a superb hunt about Gate Gills before it holed among the rocks there. Terriers worried it below and terrier Sting had to be left in all night, finally being dug out the next day.

December 15th was a grand day from Middlegill and hounds found in Parish Moss. Reynard had some narrow escapes dodging hounds as he tried to get away, but he finally got going by Watch Hill, Middlegill and then crossed to Lowca, going by the sea brows to

Harrington. They had a great hunt round Salterbeck and Moss Bay, before returning to Harrington where Charlie was eventually rolled over in Reservoir Street. He was a fine dog fox of over sixteen pounds in weight. **February 11th** was memorable in that Trixie jumped onto a crag ledge at Gate Gills and seized a fox skulking there, which she quickly finished.

March 5th was Greysouthen Hunt Ball day and they had a good hunt after finding in Dubs. Reynard then gave them a spin before going to ground in a badger sett behind Waterloo. Squick and Prince were loosed and they soon found their foe, killing it inside the sett. Another fox was worried by Squick at Burtness Combe after a fast hunt from Thunder Ghyll resulted in it going to earth. This was on **April 14th** after a meet at Scale Bridge.

A mammoth dig occurred on **April 26th** at Paper Mill Wood, Dean, and this was after terriers had been entered at 9.30am. Digging continued all day and a fifty foot narrow tunnel was dug by expert quarrymen and miners which finally reached terriers and the now dead dog fox, together with three cubs, at 8pm that night. The next day, despite such hardships, saw Willie out with his pack again at Deanscales and they dug out an old vixen in Lucetta Wood after two hours of yet more hard graft. Border Peat had killed the vixen, but she had a good commanding position and badly mauled the terrier. Half of the pack, whilst digging began, got away on another fox, a very old dog, and hunted him to Loweswater and finally killed him on Low Fell. Willie then returned to the wood the next day and dug out two cubs with the terriers. Lamb-worrying drives fell hunters on to great efforts as such killing must be stopped.

They finished the season on **May 28th** with sixty-nine foxes accounted for.

Mr and Mrs Borwick kept the Pheasant Inn at Wythop and they showed great hospitality when housing hounds, terriers and hunt staff for a week of hunting in that area and great food was always enjoyed, washed down no doubt with copious quantities of good real ale! The Pheasant has been an Inn for the past 500 years and no doubt many hunting parties have enjoyed hospitality at this ancient and charming place. The woodlands around the Inn house a good number of foxes and this area was an almost certain find. Several foxes were usually roused and hounds would often split into two or three packs, with foxes hunted all through the woods and out onto the high fells behind the Inn. There were several occasions during Irving's day when hounds hunted their fox past the old hostelry and a few of these ended with Reynard being caught close to the Inn itself. At least two hunts ended with Charlie being rolled over directly behind the Pheasant and no doubt they raised a glass or two and toasted the unfortunate 'varmints' time and again.

1943/44 SEASON

Willie began early again on **September 9th** and poor scenting conditions prevailed.

Early October saw severe floods in the fell country and by **October 12th** there was an end to them. Hounds were at Gate Gills this day and a fox was reluctant to leave the crags. Two unnamed terriers broke from Irving's side and joined in the chase, but in their eagerness they ran right over the edge of the crag and fell several feet into the branches of a lone tree that was a well-known landmark at this crag. They were coupled and hanged over each side of the branch and would surely have been throttled had not the branch broken just in time. The pair dropped into deep heather below and they were none the worse for their ordeal, much to the relief of their owner and followers.

October 29th saw them at Spedding's farm at Croasdale and this proved to be a lovely day, but with poor scent. They found about Bowness Knott, but couldn't hunt it far. They then roused one at Floutern and this went to ground after circling the tarn, at a strong rock hole under a crag and was worried below by Squick and Peggy.

November 23rd was a Buttermere hunting week and they enjoyed a long and hard hunt round Red Pike and High Stile ranges before Charlie went to earth at Bleaberry Combe. It had been a fine day, but a storm broke later on. Terriers were entered, but only one emerged, unable to get to its fox, and so Willie took hounds back to kennel and later returned to the borran near the summit of the Pike. This was quite a stronghold and terrier Major could be heard hard at his fox. The storm increased in violence and digging operations were very difficult. Such digging was carried on for the next forty-eight hours until, at last, Major was found.

He was trapped in a gryke that he had fallen into during his struggle with his foe and could not possibly have got out without assistance. They hauled him out on the Thursday, along with the fox he had accounted for, after shifting what seemed like half the fell. Willie was laid up with flu for a couple of days after this dig and this was put down to his long stint of grafting in stormy conditions.

February 1st was a good day and they made a late start due to bad weather. Reynard was away from Gate Gills and a fast hunt ensued

BACK ROW: *Maud and Willie Irving, young Maud, Harry Irving and Jack Ullock.* FRONT ROW: *Mary and Margaret (Harry's daughters) and Pearl Irving.*

round Muddick and on to Gatesgarth before Charlie went to earth not far from where he was found. Terriers Peggy and Jen were let in and they eagerly sought out and worried the fox, which wouldn't bolt from this rocky fastness.

Hounds found two foxes on Ling Fell on **April 25th** and the pack split, with two going to Sunny Brows, Darling How, Whinlatter, Swinside and then Whiteside. Singwell and Delver stuck to their pilot and pushed their fox hard over the fells until, at last, they forced it into the low country and at last killed a fine dog fox at Scalehill Hotel. The others finished at Whinlatter after losing their quarry. It had been another grand season and some shoots had also taken place, especially in the Cockermouth district. Seventy-one foxes was the final tally and quite a number of lambing calls had been answered.

Mrs Benson of the Horseshoe Inn, Lorton, was another keen supporter and hounds had met at her hostelry for decades. In the late 1930s she had already passed the eighty-four mark, yet was still providing hospitality at this comfortable country Inn. Rex of Melbreak was walked by Mrs Benson at the Horseshoe Inn and he was one of the most famous of Lakeland terriers of the 1920s and early 30s. Mrs Benson would put on large spreads for the gathering hunters and none went away hungry after a hard day among the mountains.

She retired at eighty-five years of age and was greatly missed by the Melbreak staff and followers. She was very keen on hunting with hounds and could relate many tales dating back to the time when Jonathan Banks hunted the pack. What great tales must have been lost upon the sad occasion of her death! The Horseshoe Inn is no more and the building is now a private residence. The Wheatsheaf Inn, however, remains a country pub and hounds have traditionally met here too, when hunting from Lorton. A Mr and Mrs Lennox had this place in Irving's time and they too would give great support and hospitality to the visiting hunters.

Joshua Hardisty was another stalwart of the Melbreak and he followed Jonathan Banks at every opportunity, as well as Richard Head when he took over. He also followed Irving, but was by this time getting on a bit and could no longer hunt the fells with the agility of his younger years. He was also an expert farmer and was well known in the Loweswater, Crummock and Buttermere districts. His early life had been spent as a gamekeeper at Gilgarran, then Wythop, before taking up the tenancy of Scales Farm, Lorton, where he raised his daughters and son, Sidney. He was an expert at rearing herdwick sheep and was often called upon to judge these at country shows throughout the fells. He was also a member of the hunt committee at one time and regularly walked hounds for the pack. Joshua Hardisty was the grandfather of Harry Hardisty who later became closely associated with the Melbreak Foxhounds in his own right.

Archie Bruce was another supporter and committee member and he had much in common with Willie Irving as he too was very keen on the new improved Lakeland terrier and, indeed, was one of the founder members of the Lakeland Terrier Association when it was set up in 1921 at a meeting in Keswick. He bred very smart terriers which played an important part in establishing the new type, but these were out-and-out workers that served regularly at the Melbreak. In fact, Archie Bruce could usually be found helping to dig out a fox during most hunts and his terriers saw plenty of action.

He was a pioneer of the new type of earth dog designed to be leggy and narrow enough to negotiate deep borrans and crag ledges where foxes 'bink', but even as early as 1937 he was complaining that professional show people had 'hijacked' the LTA and were now breeding mainly for show purposes alone. Bruce and his contemporaries like Douglas Paisley and Jim Dalton had started the LTA to promote a genuine, but typey, Lakeland terrier that had enough leg, coat and guts to cope with the arctic conditions of the fell country in winter, as well as the hill foxes of course. But many, especially breeders outside the fells, had no intentions of ever working their terriers and as a result the type suffered.

However, thanks to some stalwarts such as Paisley, Irving, Mrs Spence to some degree (many of her terriers were entered to fox and served for a time at the Ullswater), Bruce, Gibson and Ted Rigg, to mention but a few, working pedigree stock continued to be bred and these, thankfully, had a massive impact on strains countrywide until at least the early 1960s. After that few, if any, worked pedigree Lakeland terriers. Willie Irving complained to George Newcombe that show people had pushed working enthusiasts out of the picture, but I did not realise that this had occurred as early as 1937.

Archie Bruce told a tale of a fox that was hunted from Winscales and was killed by hounds at Lamplugh some time later. That night celebrations were held at a Distington tavern and conversation turned to the weight of the hunted fox. Three-penny guesses were made throughout the assembled company and these ranged from eighteen to twenty-six pounds, while Irving stated the fox to be fourteen and a half pounds in weight. Scales were employed and Willie was exactly right, with accusations flying that he had already weighed the fox. However, he swore he hadn't and Willie was known as a truthful man who would not tell lies. His experience had enabled him to guess the correct weight and it was he who won the money.

Archie also told a tale to illustrate how to tell a keen hunter among a crowd of youngsters. Plenty of young lads and girls followed hounds during holidays when they were in the Distington area and one day a fox was roused at Wythemoor. Hounds got away to a flying start on this fine morning and their chorus rang out in the chilled autumn air, stirring the souls of the many followers. One lad standing near Bruce said, with regard to the music of the pack, "Isn't that

Young foxes which were saved from the terriers and raised at the Kennels.

Gordon Stagg (left) with Hilton Hope and their working collies.

grand?" while a lad standing next to him stated, "Oh what a row!" Archie's brother, Jim, was a gamekeeper on the Gilgarran estate and he always welcomed hounds and made sure foxes were not eradicated in the district by over-zealous guns! Archie Bruce must rank as one of *the* most important figures in Lakeland terrier breeding and he was also keen on hound trailing, as well as hunting with hounds. He was secretary of the Melbreak pack for many years. No doubt he and Willie Irving bred many good Lakeland terriers from each other's stock during the 20s, 30s and 40s in particular.

Mrs Harrington of Branthwaite can be recounted as another very keen follower and walker of hounds and it was she who walked Cora, one of the best of the Melbreak pack during the late 1920s and through the 1930s. In fact it was Mrs Harrington who reared the bitch from being a puppy and Cora ended up spending her retirement at Branthwaite. Cracker, sadly, did not enjoy such a retirement as he was found dead in kennel one morning when Willie went to see to his pack. Cracker was a full brother to Cora and both of these hounds had hunted and killed foxes single-handed. Hillman was a son of Cora born in the 1930s and he too could hunt and kill foxes on his own.

There are many supporters I could mention and I do not like to leave any out, especially of those who kept Inns and provided great hospitality at meets, but there were literally hundreds of keen supporters and it would be impossible to mention them all.

Willie with his Lakeland terriers in the late 1940s (the terrier on the left is Mick of Millar Place).

Hunting began on **September 7th** from Swinside and they enjoyed a good hunt, but a dense mist set in which meant hounds were lost from view and the outcome was not known. **October 28th** witnessed a meet put on for the crew of HMS Melbreak at Kirkstile Inn where Mrs Stagg put on a good spread. A fox binked in Mowdy Crags and had to be left and a second went away from here and by Scale Force onto the high fells where it was lost after a good hunt.

November 1st saw a find at Palmer's Park and a good hunt ensued that went to Dean Cross, with Charlie getting onto the roof of a stable. Betty Moore chased it off and it was then rolled over on the road nearby.

November 8th was a Stockhow meet and they found on Knock and holed in what turned out to be a very bad place. G. Rowland was away fighting in the war, but he had left his terrier at the kennels to serve with hounds. Buffer was put in, but he fell into a deep rock crevice and, though they dug to the fault in the rocks, they couldn't free the terrier, despite their best efforts.

It was decided, with great reluctance, to put the poor creature down and poor Buffer was shot, dying instantly, which hopefully gave some comfort to his owner.

November 13th saw two foxes dug out using terrier Spider at Durling and both were accounted for by hounds.

Hounds met at Brigham on **November 28th** and a fox was soon afoot. They had a good hunt, but a terrific storm of wind and lashing rain broke out and they lost their fox at Cockermouth train station.

November 29th was from kennels and they hunted all day on a fox, but a cur dog spoiled the hunt late on. A few hounds had split and they had a good hunt round Swinside and holed at Boat Crag. Willie was with the other lot, so Jack Porter and Alf Turnbull climbed to the

The final season (1950/51): Willie, now in his 26th season as Huntsman, pauses with the hounds near Millar Place.

spot and Porter put in his bitch Spider. Charlie was then dug out from among the rocks and was humanely dispatched.

December 6th was at Winscales School. After losing a fox they came back by Gilgarran and found, holing it at Jackie Planting. They dug out their fox, but, sadly, lost Sting in the process, though Willie doesn't state how the poor terrier died. Possibly the fox had clamped its jaws over his nose and mouth and Sting had suffocated.

December 19th saw hounds finding on Lamplugh Fell and this fox was accounted for after quite a long hunt. A second was roused at Low Fell and gave hounds a good run until it went to ground at Bramley, with terrier Peggy quickly in action and accounting for a fine vixen.

March 21st was a good day and they enjoyed a cracking hunt at Whinlatter and up to Grisedale Pike, before hounds caught up with and killed their quarry at Thornthwaite Mines after a superb four and a half-hours of determined work.

It was during **April** of this year that Truant, whilst hunting a lamb-worrying fox, lost his footing on Mowdy Crags and fell several hundred feet from one jutting ledge to another. Fortunately this crag was full of deep heather couches and the hound hit mostly these areas, which meant, though shaken, he got away with it, avoiding serious injury and tramping back to kennels that afternoon under his own steam! This demonstrates how hardy fell hounds could be.

May 23ʳᵈ was the last day of the season, but Irving couldn't turn out. Harry Hardisty and Bob Gibson took out the pack and they accounted for a vixen on Whiteless Pike. Lambing calls had ended and the off-season began yet again, with seventy-one foxes having been accounted for. This is the first time Harry Hardisty is mentioned in Irving's diary. He was not yet the Whipper-in, but was obviously a keen follower and assisted whenever he could.

CHAPTER 11

Routine at the Kennels

It was an early start at kennels and hounds had to be cared for daily. The kennel buildings and yards were cleaned and scrubbed every day without fail and feeding time was carefully carried out, as Willie would ensure that all hounds and terriers enjoyed their fair share. Willie was known for keeping hounds in fine fettle, even during the leaner war years when feed wasn't easily come by, and after each day he would thoroughly check them over and treat any wounds they had received. At lambing time they often hunted for six or seven consecutive days and hounds were often extremely footsore, some hardly being able to walk because their pads were raw with wear. Fox and badger bites were treated thoroughly when terriers had been in action and they were not allowed to go out again until fully recovered and only when the wounds had healed properly.

After a hard day hunting in the fells, Willie would be diligent about getting in any hounds which hadn't returned when he had blown 'the gather' but if he couldn't find them, some had to be left out overnight. In such instances he would be out the next day, wandering around and blowing his horn for the missing hounds to hear.

Sometimes they were found back at the place where they had been walked as puppies; at other times they were stuck on a crag and on very rare occasions a hound was never seen again. Roads did pose a threat back then, but not as much as in more recent years. So whilst most were enjoying a restful Sunday, Willie was often out gathering in stray hounds, or searching for them among the crags, or possibly digging out a trapped terrier.

Willie began work on **September 24**[th] and was no longer single-handed as Gordon Stagg was appointed as Whipper-in by the hunt committee, though he could only help out till lambing time, as he was primarily a shepherd.

October 12th witnessed a kennels meet (where the hunt sets off from kennels) and they found on Whiteside, with hounds going to Hobcarton where they split. One lot killed in a hen house about Groves, while the others had a good hunt on Grasmoor and holed above Lanthwaite. It bolted from the terrier and was killed on the green.

October 18th was a Croasdale meet at the Spedding's farmstead and a fox was away from Banna Fell, taking hounds on a long run all the way to Loweswater, then round Melbreak and back by the post office

Willie Irving (far left) with Dalesman's (far right) pack of hounds. Mowdy Robinson is 4th from right.

to Scale Hill. Reynard kept on and went away to Lorton, only to take shelter in Jack Tyson's wash house. He was flushed out of here and was finally rolled over in Miss Musgrave's garden after giving a thrilling hunt.

November 7th witnessed a Lorton meet and the pack eventually found at Aiken Planting after a long draw. They then had a fast hunt over Whinlatter to Barf where Douglas Paisley was in at the kill. Although honorary Whipper-in at the Blencathra, he also hunted with the Melbreak whenever possible.

Willie was lamed on **January 3**[rd] whilst looking for a hound at Gasgale Ghyll and Jack Ullock took over hunting hounds for a day or two, with Gordon assisting. Fell Hounds Stormer and Towley hunted and killed a fox on **January 27**[th] at Hill Farm.

March 13th was at Lamplugh Green and hounds marked an earth in a nearby wood. Terriers were entered and then Willie dug out a large sow badger, while the terriers worried her youngsters before they were reached.

Hounds were called out to Rogerscale on **April 2**[nd] after poultry had been worried by a fox. They roused a little dog fox and hunted it on to the high end of Dodd, where they at last had the chicken thief.

April 9th was a call-out for lamb-worrying at Kirkgate and they had a good hunt after hitting a drag round the pastures and killed an old dog fox at the bottom of Red Ghyll.

May 3rd was yet another lambing call at Rigg House and three fine cubs were dug out at Saw Mill Ghyll, with an old dog fox being dug out of an earth at Pit Wood. That seems to have put an end to lambing troubles which finished untypically early that year, with forty-nine foxes having been caught over the course of that season.

Some hunting days were incredibly long and this often meant that Willie returned to kennels after dark, whether at Millar Place, or at a temporary base in a residence in the area being hunted for the week. One hunt lasted twelve hours in total and if they hit off at 9.30am, this meant they didn't finish until 9.30pm. Hounds would then have to be taken back to kennels and fed and bedded down, with injuries treated, including those found on any terriers that had been to ground. And then, and only then, did Willie see to himself. This meant that he was sometimes late for hunt balls and other social events held after a day

ABOVE: *Young Maud hoping to make a whipper-in!*
RIGHT: *Pearl with a Melbreak hound.*

on the fells, but he was always made very welcome. Fell Huntsmen have been held in great esteem for decades, maybe even centuries in the Lake District and those attending such functions always wished to see them among the assembled company.

This gruelling twelve-hour hunt has to be one of the longest on record, but it is not *the* longest overall. That distinction goes to the Eskdale and Ennerdale Foxhounds during Tommy Dobson's time as Huntsman. In the spring of 1890 'laal' Tommy's pack roused their fox at 6.30am during a lambing call and this chap proved to be a real hardy hill fox who led hounds a 'merry dance' all over the high and low country and kept them going all day and into the evening, whilst always keeping ahead of them. After a testing and exhausting hunt, hounds eventually pulled down their fox at 11.30 that night after an incredible and record hunt of seventeen hours. They may have changed foxes during the hunt, or maybe it was the same one, it is impossible to know, but this must be a record that still stands today. Willie had many hunts that lasted all day and sometimes ended after dark, but his longest was the twelve-hour hunt mentioned earlier. It must have been exhausting in those days, for hounds would have to be walked back to kennels after a hard hunt like that, though sometimes, especially if darkness had fallen, hunt servants, hounds and terriers would head for the nearest farm and they would be sure to find a bed and other home comforts at such residences.

1946/47 SEASON

A start was made on **September 23rd** and Willie reports that they "had a nice hunt with a fox that holed and was killed by terriers in Whiteless Breast."

November 1st saw hounds meet at Lanthwaite (thwaite is pronounced 'thert' in fell parlance). They found a fox skulking at Red Ghyll Edge and then enjoyed a grand hunt round Grasmoor. Gordon Stagg (he was no longer able to be Whipper-in due to farm duties, though he still assisted whenever possible) and Jack Porter, were not far behind and they found hounds marking at Dove Crags. Gordon had Vic by this time, the black and tan Lakeland given him by Willie (there is currently a photograph of this terrier in the bar of the Bridge Hotel, Buttermere, standing next to a collie and Gordon himself) just after the war. Vic was game and they dug out the fox using this terrier. He was so useful, in fact, that he served under Harry Hardisty when he Whipped-in to, and then hunted, the Melbreak.

They were at Sunny Brows on **November 19th** and found almost immediately, with Reynard going away to the heights of Whinlatter. Here they split on a number of foxes and several hunts ensued. The only kill was with two hounds, Remedy and Betty, who accounted for one of the foxes at Thwaites Planting.

March 26th witnessed hounds drawing Low Fell and they enjoyed a good hunt that crossed to Melbreak, where they had a grand run until, finally, Reynard was so hard pressed that he ran into the old kennel buildings at the ex-Banks farm and was killed there.

Hounds met at Lorton on **March 31st** and they accounted for one fox near Brown How. Remedy and Barmaid got away on a second fox and had a good hunt up Brackenthwaite, round Whiteside and back, only to hole at Hope Ghyll. Terriers worried it below as it refused to bolt.

The steep cleft of Sour Milk Ghyll, scene of many of Irving's hunts.

An old and rare photo of De Courcy-Parry (the author 'Dalesman') seen here hunting in the Fells.

April 8th was a sopping wet day with pouring rain and hounds hit a drag to Low Fell, after a meet at Deanscales, then had several good hunts. They holed one at Lorton and got it and a badger out of the earth, though the terriers had quite a time of it and took a bit of a mauling from the badger before finally being dug out. Badgers underground can present great challenges to terriers, and will fight ferociously. Foxes have been known to hide behind badgers in an earth, leaving the badger to face the terrier.

On **April 20th** fell hound Stormer hunted a fox on his own for a long distance on a wild and wet stormy day. He started near Lanthwaite and ended up catching his fox at Step Ghyll after a long run that had taken in quite a few of the high fells.

April 29th was a lambing call and hounds marked at Durling, where Willie dug out a vixen and four cubs. Stormer yet again had one up on his own and Gordon took off in pursuit of this hunt, which ended with Reynard going to earth at Oak Bank. Here Gordon dug out a fine dog fox worried by his terrier Vic and the lamb-killers were 'brought to book'. Willie had given Gordon the terrier Vic on Victory Day when still a puppy and he grew into a superb finder and a hard killer of any fox that wouldn't bolt.

May 2nd was another good day and this, it seems, was another effort to catch up with lamb-worriers, meeting early at Hope Farm. They found on Swinside and had a very fast hunt round Hobcarton and Grisedale and succeeded in killing a fine dog fox near the Holdings. Another hunt at Grisedale ended with a kill among the forestry workers under Grisedale Pike, while a third hunt was in progress. This led to Combe and Thornthwaite where it ended with Charlie going into the old lead mines, with half the pack following, though some didn't return and Willie only found out on Sunday where they were. Willie, along with a few helpers, arrived at the mines and went in to rescue them, with hounds being found safe and well, alongside the carcass of a fine dog fox they had killed in the mine.

The last hunt was **May 13th** and Willie lost touch with hounds as they disappeared into the mist and rain and thus failing to add to the seasonal tally of fifty-one foxes killed.

Chapter 12

A New Whip

It was during the off-season of 1947 that Harry Hardisty was appointed as Whipper-in. He had already hunted with the Melbreak for several seasons and had assisted Willie whenever he could, so he knew the country well and had already proved useful with both hounds and terriers. No doubt he learnt much from watching Irving at work and this stood him in good stead for when he would take over as Huntsman in a few years' time. Willie and Harry got on well. Harry and local shepherd and temporary whipper-in Gordon Stagg were great friends too, both having worked as shepherds and sharing a keen interest in fell hunting.

Gordon and Harry were both courting Buttermere lasses at the same time and they would often travel down into this remote valley in order to meet them at the Fish Hotel for the evening. Gordon tells amusing tales of this pair of rogues 'borrowing' boats from the Crummock jetty in order to save a bit of leg work. It was either walk all the way, or take a boat and row the length of Crummock water, which would put them within easy walking distance of the hostelry. The only trouble was, the wind often howled down the valley and this meant that boating on the lake was very often a case of getting nowhere fast, no matter how hard they rowed, hacking at the choppy waters like madmen!

Gordon tells a hilarious tale of a night out with Harry and their respective wives. They attended a wedding at Hundith Hill Hotel and left about midnight, taking the girls home to the kennels first, before heading back to the Horse Shoe Inn for 'after hours'. After a couple of drinks they came out and a fella was having difficulty starting his van, so Gordon and Harry gave kind assistance and soon got him on his way, the van spluttering off into the distance in a cloud of exhaust fumes. It was just as he went out of sight, rounding some dark and distant bend, that Gordon and Harry realised it was **their** van he had stolen, along with their help! The police found the van the next day in the middle of a field at Scales. A farm worker had obviously 'borrowed' it to save himself a long walk, much the same as they had 'borrowed' a boat from Crummock jetty on numerous occasions. Maybe it was the owner of the boat getting his own back!

De Courcy-Parry (on white horse) at the John Peel centenary in 1954.

Willie loosed from kennels on **September 20th**, starting off the new season, and a good hunt was enjoyed after several foxes were afoot from Dodd. Hounds split and one lot went by Hobcarton to Whinlatter and lost their fox in the woods there, whilst a second fox was hunted by Ragman alone from Hobcarton right along the tops to Whiteside. In by Low House Crags they raced and to ground there, where the terriers worried a fine dog fox.

November 4th witnessed a meet at Wythop Hall and they had a grand hunt through dense woodland, with terriers helping to flush it from thick cover at times, before getting it out into the open and killing on the shores of Bassenthwaite Lake near the toll bar.

December 9th was a Peel Wyke meet and they had a fox away that took them the whole length of the woods and up the low bottoms as far as Braithwaite before finally killing in Mr Dixon's garden at Thornthwaite after a good run.

December 22nd saw hounds drawing Carling Knott and they enjoyed a very good day. One fox went over Carling Knott to Melbreak and across to Low Fell and was killed in Foulsyke Barn. One fox binked several times before going to ground and being worried by the terriers on Melbreak Fell. Meanwhile Delver went away on his own trail and his hunt took him all over Red Pike Range before heading into low-lying land with Reynard being caught in the ice-cold waters of Buttermere Lake. A third fox crossed to Low Fell in the afternoon and kept hounds running until after dark. A very hard, long day.

December 29th was a wild snowy morning and they drew Dodd and Whiteside without finding, so Irving called hounds off as it was such a bad day.

January 21st was a bitter cold day with a very hard frost and they again failed to find in such bad conditions.

February 10th witnessed a Rogerscale meet and the day was very wet indeed. Hounds failed to find, but Harry himself spotted a fox lying in on Mosser Fell and dug it out, probably using Gordon's terrier, Vic.

March 19th was a very wet and misty morning and Willie decided to call them off when the mist descended and became even more dense.

Hounds were once again at Carling Knott on **March 22nd** and they had a long hunt round Fangs, back by Carling Knott, Black Crag and Hencombe, only to hole at Blea Crag. The terrier bolted the fox quickly and the hunt took hounds to Buttermere where they killed on the doorstep of the vicarage after being all round the village.

Hounds had a week at Buttermere during **April** and poor Rockwood, a very good young hound, was killed when he fell from Honister Crag, a place that has claimed the lives of a number of Lakeland hounds over the years. The hunting had been of the very best, but this sad loss marred the occasion.

May 2nd was a lambing call and they came across a likely earth, but dug three badgers out instead of the expected fox. The badger population seemed to be increasing after the war and Willie dug quite a number of badgers during this season.

May 7th saw hounds at Gatesgarth in search of a lamb-worrier and a fox ran from Gate Gills to Robinson and went to earth at Hackney Holes. Jewel and Tony were entered and they worried the fox below ground. This was the last hunt that season and brought the number up to seventy-one foxes accounted for.

CHAPTER 13

The Myth of Turk

Much has been spoken and written of Turk of Melbreak (1930–32), but this chapter concerns another terrier Irving is supposed to have bred in the early 1950s after he had resigned from his post as Huntsman. This terrier was said to be not only a grand-looking terrier but a real terror: a bad fighter that would kill any other dog that upset him. Even Brian Plummer mentions this terrier in his book, *The Fell Terrier*, stating that he was a son of Oregill Copper Coin, but my research has dispelled yet more myths about another of Willie's many earth dogs.

First of all, Turk was not bred after Willie had left his post as Huntsman, but was bred at the end of the 1930s and Turk began serving at the hunt possibly in 1941 when we have the first mention of him, though this could possibly have been his second season. Willie's daughters Pearl and Maud cannot remember this dog and they state that their father held the name of Turk to be sacred to his famous earlier dog which had died and that he would not have given the name to another. However, Willie did not name the dog. It was either Jack or Frank Pepper who bought this dog from Willie, but he served at the Melbreak throughout the 1940s after Irving had probably purchased the dog back, which wasn't an uncommon occurrence.

Champion Zip, belonging to Bob Gibbons, mated My Pride and produced Kupid of Kinniside. Mountain Pride, possibly Irving's terrier, mated his bitch Meg and this produced Whiskers, which Maud can remember at the hunt. Kupid of Kinniside then mated Whiskers and this produced the mythical and legendary Turk already described, though his full name was Bowder Stone Turk, which tells us that Pepper had this dog and named him as a puppy. He then either sold the dog back to Willie, or loaned him almost permanently, whilst no doubt keeping the stud rights. What is certain is that he had nothing to do with Copper Coin and was born years before this dog.

His first appearance in the hunting diaries is on September 17th 1941 and this was a hunt at Carling Knott. Two foxes were put off and one gave a superb hunt to Herdus and then came back by Croasdale to where the old Knock mine used to be, where one went to ground. Turk and Rock, eager to go, were loosed from their couples and they quickly found, seizing their fox and killing it before it was finally dug out and proved to be a fine dog fox. Turk was only a young dog at this time, but was already showing that he was quality and such abilities would make him yet another legend at the hunt. He then went on to serve throughout the 1940s and was still in action at the end of this decade. Irving often used his terriers into old age as many Lakelands wore very well indeed and could give as many as twelve or thirteen seasons in some cases. It was Bowder Stone Turk who sired Burtness Lady in the early 1940s when put to Old Peggy.

It was not true that he was a bad fighter and easily offended, as is seen by the fact that he was put to ground with another male, Rock, to tackle a fox and nobody in their right mind would put an aggressive dog to ground with even a bitch, let alone another male. However, there were two other Turks at the hunt during the 1940s, though they belonged to followers, probably having been bred by Irving and sold as puppies. So the mystery and myth of Turk is at last settled.

1948/49 season

September 20th started the season off and hounds had a good hunt on Whiteside and holed on Dodd, with the terriers worrying the fox before it could be dug out.

November 2nd saw hounds at Elva Plain and Willie cast off in the woods. They had a good day, despite the wild and wet conditions. One fox was killed at Long Bottom. Then hounds joined up with a group called the Troutbeck Lodge Hounds, and went on to kill a fox under Redmain, with another suspected kill behind Old Hewthwaite. Another was run to ground near Jonathan Planting and was dug out and accounted for with both packs in attendance.

November 9th witnessed a meet at Wythop Hall and plenty of foxes were astir in the woods, with a number of deer afoot too. Ragman killed a fox by himself on the road near Beck Wythop.

They were at the Horse Shoe Inn on **November 13th** on a very misty day, but scenting was good. Delver ran and killed on his own near Rash Wood and Laddie also got away on his own, having a fast and long hunt that took in the high tops and he finally killed his fox near Beck House. Yet another fox was hunted and then killed near the top of Rising Sun. A superb and thrilling day with wonderful hound work of the very best on display.

The traditional Shepherds' Meet was on **November 26th** and hounds found at Scaw Crags after drawing for some time and distance. During this hunt, which petered out at Dove Crags, Careful had a great hunt on her own with a second fox that took in Whiteless and Rannerdale Knott and she finally killed it near Rannerdale after a superb solo performance.

January 28th witnessed a fast hunt from Sour Milk Ghyll to High Stile, High Crag and on to Haystacks, with the fox then coming back, only to go to earth under High Stile. Faulder of Buttermere was on the spot with his terriers and he dug and drew out the fox, setting it on its feet again. Hounds pulled down a fine dog fox soon after.

April 9th was a meet at the Kirkstile Inn and they quickly had several foxes stirring on Melbreak Fell. Willie Porter and a number of Eskdale and Ennerdale followers were in attendance and they witnessed a good hunt that saw a fox bink in Ling Crag, before being flushed out, only to go to earth in Low Dale. The terriers bolted him and he was rolled over by hounds near Scale Beck.

May 1st saw Harry Hardisty in charge at Buttermere and hounds had a long hunt on a fox that binked in Buxom Hows before going on to Gable Crag where Charlie binked again. He was flushed out and hounds had him soon after. Unfortunately two good hounds, Dainty and Ranger, whilst in the process of attempting to reach the fox, fell from the crag and were both killed. The last lamb-worrying call was on **May 22nd** and they successfully ended the troubles, finishing the season with eighty-one adult foxes accounted for.

Willie following the Blencathra Foxhounds with Jorrocks, 1956.

CHAPTER 14

Fundraising and Social Events

Willie Irving was an outgoing and sociable fellow and he had a certain presence about him which made any social event just that little more enjoyable when he was in attendance. Only illness, or a very late finish to hunting, could keep Willie away from his evening socials and in those days there were plenty going on. Hunt balls were a favourite of his and these were put on in the district in which hounds were hunting for that week. Distington (the Empress Ballrooms) where Jack Jackson and his Thirlmere Band entertained with hunting songs, Cockermouth, Lamplugh, Whitehaven, Loweswater, Greysouthen, Buttermere, Dean, to name but a few, were places where hunt balls took place, as well as other fundraising events. These were usually very well attended and as many as five hundred plus were at some of the larger venues such as the one at Distington, which attracted folk from all over the Melbreak country, including farmers, villagers and townsfolk too. Workington, Whitehaven and all surrounding villages were represented at these balls and they raised much-needed funds. Lorton also put on a hunt ball and Billy Hill, a farmer from near Lorton, used to play the piano for the dances and he later wrote a song about Willie (see appendix 1). It can truthfully be stated that Irving's popularity saw more and more fundraising committees being set up and each held hunt balls, whist drives, dances and country shows in order to raise money to keep hounds hunting.

One of the hunt balls of 1937 was at Embleton and music for the dancing was provided by the Broughton Gaiety Band, with two duets being sung by Mr Skelton (tenor) and Mr Kenolon (bass). The prizes for Spot Waltzes were won by Mr Gaskell, Miss Moore, Mr Skelton and Miss Edmunds, which were presented by Mrs Leathes. Among the winners of the whist drives was local journalist and author 'Dalesman'

(De Courcy-Parry) who was a very keen and ardent hunter and a good friend of Irving's. A Mr Peart entertained at many Hunt Balls.

There was also a Miss Melbreak competition and different venues were used throughout the Melbreak country in order to select winners for the final, which was usually judged by, among others, Willie Irving himself (not an easy job, but someone had to do it!). All of these events raised capital to keep hounds and hunt staff in action and the Melbreak enjoyed a very healthy balance sheet during Irving's time in particular. His popularity drew in crowds to both the hunting field and social events and this kept funds coming in fast and furious each season, with record funds being raised on occasion.

Car followers increased to large numbers as the years went by and these gave great financial support to the hunt too, though Willie was dismayed to see some young men among this throng. He believed car following was great for the elderly, but that the young should get their boots on and get out onto those fells.

BELOW: *Miss Eskdale & Ennerdale receives her sash. Willie Irving (left) was among the judges.* OPPOSITE: *With friends at the HTA.*

1949/50 SEASON

It was a warm start on **September 25th** and scent was surprisingly good, with a kill in the beck at Bar Yeat. Jobby's Hunt (see page 191) on **November 14th** saw hounds having a good hunt on an old fox that went away by Scale Force and to the Red Pike district, eventually running hounds off on High Crag.

February 22nd witnessed hounds drawing Hay and they had a good hunt here, with Reynard going to ground on Hay Breast. Turk, now towards the end of his career, was put in and bedlam ensued, with Turk hard at his quarry, not allowing it to bolt. Willie dug like a fiend and eventually came upon his old dog who was tackling two adult foxes at the same time. Irving got both of them, but his terrier had received quite a mauling for his troubles, refusing to give an inch in the face of a vicious onslaught and having killed at least one of the foxes before he was dug out.

This experience demonstrates just how game Turk was and why he too had become a legend at the Melbreak.

March 8th was at Close Breast and they had a fast hunt that resulted in Reynard running to earth at Andrew Bank. Vic (Stagg's terrier) and Brant were entered and they worried their foe below ground. Brant of Lorton was the sire of Distington Lass, a registered Lakeland which Billy sold to Albert Thomas. She became the dam of Irving's Reminder ('pet' name Gill) when put to Oregill Peter, a son of Oregill Copper Coin. The dam of Distington Lass was Gill of Millar Place.

April 13th witnessed hounds drawing Melbreak Fell and they had a fast hunt from Mowdy Crags, which went twice round Melbreak and then away, going via Burnbank all the way to Lamplugh and they at last caught up with their fox, killing it under a car in Sid Bruce's garage at Mill Gill Head.

April 16th saw Harry and Willie taking separate packs to hunt down lamb killers and Irving dug out a vixen and cubs at Swinside End,

whilst Hardisty took his hounds to Buttermere and had a grand hunt from Gable Crag, which ended in the killing of a dog fox near Low Snab. Hounds hunted a fox to Hackney Holes and Irving dug out a fine dog fox that had also been killing lambs. This ended the season with seventy foxes accounted for.

LEFT: *This horn was presented to Willie on his leaving the Melbreak. It is battered and bruised after much use and is still in the family.*

CHAPTER 15

Jobby's Hunt

The Melbreak Foxhounds had for decades included in their fixtures the strangely named 'Jobby's Hunt' and this was held on Martinmas Monday every year without fail. Jobby Beck was the Loweswater Blacksmith for many years during the time Jonathan Banks hunted hounds and he was such a keen hunter and supporter of the Melbreak that he was given the privilege on this day of saying where hounds should be loosed and his favourite spots were Foulsyke and Low Fell where, invariably, they quickly had a fox going.

It was in 1943 that 'Athy' Swinburn boasted that he had never missed this special fixture since the day it was inaugurated and he was nearly eighty at the time and still following on foot. His pace was still quick enough to get him to the right place at the right time and he knew a good hound as well as anybody.

Jobby was a skilled Blacksmith and his forge, unless he was holding court from the Inn at Kirkstile, was always full of farmers and shepherds having a chat whenever they had time to spare. He

At Loweswater Smithy: (left to right) J. Norman, 'Jobby' Beck and Jonathan Banks.

was also Sexton of the little church, Assistant Overseer, Income Tax Collector (which didn't seem to detract from his popularity!) and Parish Lawyer. He never turned out in his working clothes outside working hours but always went home and 'scrubbed up' first. He was frequently found in the bar of the Kirkstile Inn during the evenings, but he was always in his best clothes and washed and clean-shaven. He also drank moderately and was never seen to be drunk. All in all he was a good fellow and as keen as any man when it came to supporting his local pack of hounds.

Willie and his pack moving off from Cockermouth at the start of his final season. The near-black terrier is Jim, brother of Wear's Tear 'Em, and Barker's Judy.

CHAPTER 16

The Final Season: 1950/51

Whilst still hunting hounds, Willie had been assisting the secretary of the Hound Trailing Association on a part-time basis and this post was about to become available full-time, as the then-secretary was due to retire. The HTA, impressed with Willie's hard work and people skills, offered him the job and no doubt he had much thinking to do. He loved his hounds and his terriers and still greatly enjoyed his hunting, but he was now in his early 50s and the job was getting more and more demanding.

He had sustained a few injuries during his time at the hunt and no doubt these old wounds bothered him to some degree, especially after a long and tiring day. In his early days he could climb those fells without breaking into a sweat and walk the tops and valleys all day long without fuss, but he was now getting older and keeping up with his beloved hounds was becoming more difficult. He felt that fell pack hunting was a young man's job and that this was the right time for him to get out and let a young man take over.

He thought things through and then sat his family down and told them his decision, whilst giving good reasons for it. His decision to resign from the hunt and take up the post with the HTA must have been a difficult one, both for himself and his family. After explaining his reasons, however, he was fully supported in his decision and the 1950/51 season, his 26th, would be his last at his beloved 'Laal' Melbreak. Leaving the charming and beautifully situated house at Millar Place must have been a hard and bitter pill to swallow for all concerned, but at least his work with the HTA would still involve hounds.

His decision was made easier by the fact that, since he had taken over as Huntsman, the financial and social side of the hunt, and especially the support from farmers (the most important support of all), had increased to such a degree that left the hunt in a very strong and confident position. Also, the pack of hounds he had bred along solid lines over the past quarter of a century were very efficient indeed and this is borne out by his hunting diaries, as well as the remarkable number of hounds that could hunt and kill a fox alone and unaided, which we have only touched on throughout this book. And, importantly, Willie had trained a good and reliable young Whipper-in, in the art of hunting hounds and working terriers and Irving felt that his beloved pack were in safe hands, which was a compliment to Harry Hardisty who would go on to enjoy great success at the hunt too. It was for these reasons that Willie thought it the right time to go, but that didn't ease the blow for the followers themselves.

Farmers, shepherds, miners, quarrymen, villagers, townspeople – all were rather downhearted at the news of Willie's coming departure and even Major Iredale, the Master, tried to keep him there in at least some capacity. He and the committee offered him a Joint-Mastership to be taken up after he left his post, but Willie, though flattered, declined, concluding that he couldn't do the role justice because of his many duties with the HTA. The Major and Committee members disagreed, but he couldn't be swayed and graciously turned down such a noble and generous offer.

Willie's last season, therefore began on **September 25th** and hounds drew Scalehill Woods, with mist and rain quickly setting in. Hounds enjoyed a good hunt on Howes and over to Whiteside, where Charlie holed in the top of Hazel Ghyll. Terriers worried this fox below ground. A second was killed above ground close to the top of Gasgale Ghyll and was picked up by visitors.

October 8th was at Gate Gills and scent was poor. Willie called off as the weather rapidly deteriorated and heavy rain and hail poured from the lowering skies. **October 14th** witnessed hounds drawing the steep screes of Whiteside and they found at Boat Crag, with a good hunt

Willie stands next to Harry Hardisty, his successor as Huntsman, at the Kirkstile Inn meet.

following, that saw Reynard hole at Lanthwaite Field. He was bolted by the terriers and then holed again in Whiteside Breast. Terriers quickly found and bolted him again, but the hound Monty was soon on his brush, pulling him down as he tried to jump the fell wall.

The pack was at Cockermouth on **January 9th** and they hunted in very cold, snowy weather. Hounds had a good hunt on Hay and holed in a drain at Organ Wells. Terriers were put in and they worried their fox, which wouldn't bolt and face hounds again.

They were at Sunny Brows on **March 19th** and the weather was cold, but dry. The pack hunted and killed one fox at Darling How. They had a second going on Swinside before killing what turned out to be an old dog fox at Thwaites.

It was a wild and bitterly cold day when they drew Melbreak Fell on **March 21st** and they found near the old kennels. This fox gave them a good hunt before climbing onto Pillar Rake where it binked among the crags. Two hounds tried to reach Reynard, but they lost their footing and fell a long distance, but, miraculously, were unhurt; just a little shaken. The weather turned even worse, so Willie called hounds off and returned them to kennels.

Hounds met at Dean on **March 26th**, Easter Monday, and they found in Jackie Planting, with this fox taking them all the way to the heights of Carling Knott where it went to ground. Meanwhile the clouds had tumbled in and the wind whipped up into a fury, with a raging snow blizzard breaking out so that they were forced to leave the fox below ground and return to where hounds were kennelled for the week, near Dean.

April 1st started a day for good hunting, but bad weather interfered yet again. Hounds found on Whinlatter and their fox took them out over the wild heights of Hobcarton and right over the bleak fell tops covered in snow, then dropped into the Newlands Valley, where the hunt ended without the result known as another snow blizzard broke out and made keeping in touch impossible.

May 9th witnessed hounds hunting the Buttermere area in response to lamb losses and they had a good hunt that took them through low-

lying fields to Scale, along by Burtness to Scarf and then they made for Fleetwith Pike. Their pilot then took them up onto Honister and over

Tess, out of Trim, and a superb-looking terrier.

into Borrowdale. Reynard took them by Seatoller and Seathwaite and then back over Honister, now going at a cracking pace down the dale. They went round into Warscale now and there killed a fine vixen that wasn't suckling cubs. Willie referred to these as 'geld' vixens. A few hounds then took up an old drag that led to a hole under Moulds and a vixen and three cubs were dug out, but they had already been worried by the terriers.

May 13th was William Irving's last outing as Huntsman and this, as usual at this time of year, was a lambing call. They were at Rigg House at first light and Willie dug out four cubs in Jackie Planting and all had been worried by the terrier before they could be reached. It was quite a walk back to kennels that day and one can imagine the mixed feelings Willie must have felt as he tramped those lonely miles home with his pack of stout-hearted hounds milling about him, his shackled terriers proudly walking alongside their master, for the last time as Huntsman of the famous Melbreak Foxhounds.

He must have looked to the heights all around and remembered great hunts through the many glorious seasons, with the music of hounds swelling to full cry and the yapping bay of his many terriers to earth resounding from the craggy fellsides and deep-cut valleys, recalled the cheers and holloers of followers ringing out in the chilly winter air of many years gone by. And then he must at last have reached home, his beloved Millar Place where he had spent many happy years, raising his family and enjoying unlimited hunting to the full.

There had been some hard times true, even one or two close shaves in which he might have lost his life, like the time two hounds on couples knocked him down Gasgale Ghyll leaving him badly injured. Willie blew his hunting horn and fortunately Jack Ullock heard and instinctively knew something was wrong. He went to investigate and then helped Willie down off the fell. But with all the knocks and triumphs behind him, Willie could rightfully bask in the knowledge and satisfaction that he had done the local farmers and shepherds a very good turn in controlling such a ruthless and highly efficient predator for so long. Even during his final season he had accounted

The 1951 Presentation marking the moment Willie retired from his long service as Huntsman of the Melbreak.

for seventy adult foxes and he must have been very pleased with such a successful outcome. His twenty-sixth season had been a mixed one of bad weather and poor scenting, but still most days had been highly successful and the terriers had enjoyed an exceptionally busy year.

On his retirement Willie was presented with his battered and bruised hunting horn that had been inscribed with the words: Melbreak 1951 – Presented to Willie Irving on his retirement after 25 years devoted service, together with a testimonial from 809 members and friends. Those members and friends were listed and, though the majority were in his hunt country, some were from places throughout the Lake District and beyond.

The writer 'Dalesman' paid him a great compliment in saying that Willie had done more for the Lakeland terrier than any one else and he was also considered a great ambassador for fell hunting. Such tributes touched Willie deeply and he would never forget them.

CHAPTER 17

Working for the Hound Trailing Association

The Irving family moved from Millar Place, Lorton, to Prospect House at Cockermouth and Willie and his wife Maud were able to buy this elegant residence simply because they had managed their finances with great efficiency over the years. Willie had his office in one of the front rooms overlooking the garden and his kennel was situated along the outer wall of the garden. He may not have been Huntsman any longer, but he still kept, worked and bred his refined strain of Lakeland terrier that had successfully worked some of the deepest and most dangerous borrans to be found in the north. He supplied many show terriers at this time, but his stock were also workers and they went to hunts and terrier lads throughout the country. The author, Brian Plummer, could remember terriermen from his own South Welsh valleys travelling to Cockermouth during the 1950s in order to purchase Lakeland terriers from Irving for fox and badger digging.

He had appeared in a radio show sometime towards the end of the war years and he began by saying that he was single-handed in kennel and had been throughout the war, being the Huntsman, Kennelman and Whipper-in all in one, though he acknowledged that Maud, his wife, was always very keen on hunting and gave her husband all the support he could need. He appeared on radio again in 1956 and gave an interesting and witty interview in defence of hunting, dispelling some of the myths surrounding foxes and their habits. I listened to a recording of this interview and was fascinated to be listening to a man I have been researching and writing about for several years.

Willie took up his secretarial work for the HTA and quickly became a great success, fulfilling his post as eagerly as he had hunted his hounds. Hound trailing, in which a pack followed a pre-set scent trail, had grown in popularity, but he was determined to establish this sport further and build a much more solid support-base throughout the country and in Ireland.

The origins of this sport are surrounded in mystery and one theory holds that the Vikings brought with them their great hunting hounds and that these were responsible for bringing hound trailing to the fells. Another theory suggests that the sport began at the beginning of the 19th century and that fell pack Huntsmen first began trailing during the summer off-season, impatient of waiting for the autumn to come round again. My money would be on the latter theory as the Vikings are known more for bringing herding dogs to our shores and it was likely the Celts who first introduced hounds to the British Isles. The Vikings were great farmers and shepherds and were also probably responsible for, if not introducing, the Herdwick, at least creating it from stock they brought with them.

LEFT: *Willie judging Lakelands. He was later asked to judge at Crufts.*
ABOVE: *Lord Lonsdale, Ernie Towers and Willie Irving judging at Grasmere. Towers provided terriers for the Coniston Pack and these were partly bred from Irving-strain Lakelands.*

Prospect House, Cockermouth, to which Willie and Maud moved on retirement.

In the early days most foot packs in the fells did not have either kennels, or professional Huntsmen and farmers all came together and assisted hounds whenever possible. So it was owners of hounds intent on having the fleetest of the pack, rather than professional hunt servants, who would have begun trailing with their charges out of season and the carcass of a fox, a hare, or even a polecat or pine marten, was likely used, as hounds hunted a variety of quarry in those days. As time went by, longer trails were laid and this needed a stronger scent, so aniseed oil mixed with paraffin has become the favoured scent in more recent times. Even aniseed mixed with engine oil is used in wet conditions, in order to make scent more holding.

There has been much debate as to which are faster: trail hounds, or those that hunt foxes. They share the same ancestry in reality, but the sheer hardiness and fitness of those hunting foxes on the fells may well give them the edge.

This was demonstrated by Ruby, one of Tommy Dobson's hounds that, after hunting through the winter, won trails all over the Lake District and she was almost unbeatable. Willie Porter also tried his hounds, Rally, Bowler and Cleaver, in a trail at Eskdale. They finished the trail in that exact order, gaining first, second and third prizes. John Jackson, the famous 19th century Huntsman of the Holcombe Hunt, when they were kennelled just below the Shoulder of Mutton Inn at Holcombe Village, also used his hunting hounds for summer trails held in the Pennines and his stuff was also unbeatable.

Sunset, one of the greatest of all trail hounds, was the son of Champ, of the Blencathra Foxhounds. Longship was another great winner and this hound was out of Eskdale and Ennerdale stock. This hound took over 120 first prizes, an incredible achievement. So perhaps hounds that were hunted, or sons and daughters of hunting hounds, have proved to be the quickest.

Willie was a great ambassador for the sport of trailing and as each season passed, the morale of the Association and its members improved greatly and his popularity brought in more and more members. He helped establish hound trailing on a much more solid footing in Ireland and one of his great ambitions was to found international trails at Lowther, which he successfully accomplished towards the end of his time at the HTA. In fact, the first international trails were held in conjunction with his testimonial upon his retirement from the association and they were a great success.

The HTA was founded in about 1907 when the first recorded meeting was held in Whitehaven on March 14th of that year. The

Irving (right) and fellow judges checking the HTA trophies.

Outside the Pheasant Hotel, Bassenthwaite in 1957: (left to right) J. Redmond, the Captain of HMS Melbreak and his wife, Emily Redmond and Major Iredale.

first AGM was on January 24th 1908 at an unrecorded location, but the 1909 AGM was held at Egremont. The very first championship was won by Mrs Dickinson's Duster in 1909. From then on the HTA went from strength to strength and Irving helped to make the support base much more solid. One of the things that did threaten the sport, however, was cheating. This was only carried out by a small minority, but still, such practises could threaten the future of hound trailing, so Willie, as well as others, did their utmost to stamp it out.

One method of cheating was to have someone waiting on the fell top with an identical hound to the one released at the start of the trail. This would be released at the fell top ahead of the rest, as they approached, and the identical starting hound would be caught and taken away. The fresh hound would then win easily and the prize and money made from gambling would be theirs. The only way to prevent this was to catch them in the act and one or two have been caught and prosecuted over the years. Another method was for the trail layer to lift the scent for a good distance, then drop it again, leaving a gap. Information would have been leaked as to where the trail was being laid and a hound would have been walked over the course the day before. When this hound came to the gap in scent, it would know exactly where to go, while the others would be baffled and take a few minutes to find where the trail could be taken up again.

Ready for the off! The trail has been set and the local trail hounds are eager to be let loose.

One such trail layer was suspected of this and Willie, together with a friend, set off for the fell tops in order to catch him in the act. Two trails were being laid that day and Willie fixed on his man and climbed the fells in pursuit, hoping to catch him 'at it'. The only trouble was he had followed the wrong man and groaned inwardly when he saw John Cowen coming across the fell with his trail laid behind him. He knew then he had followed the wrong chap and the suspected cheat was left to his own devices and would have to be followed on another day.

Difficulties did arise and such were Willie's abilities that he usually succeeded in keeping everyone happy, especially landowners and farmers over whose terrain the trails led, and he was constantly writing letters in furtherance of the sport. Hound trailing became even more popular in Ireland and Willie made trips out there to help get it more established. His retirement in 1964 at the trails at Lowther was met with regret by the HTA, but Irving had surely earned the right to slow down a little by this time. He was an incredibly active and busy man and still lived life to the full, giving as much support

to the Melbreak as he could, as the welfare of his old hunt remained
dear to him.

He had found it difficult to hunt with the Melbreak during that
first season Harry Hardisty was in charge, simply because hounds
still knew him and they would rush up to him, rather baffled at his
not hunting them. However, in time they knew Harry was in charge
and he could then follow them regularly again. He also hunted with
all of the other fell packs, as well as more distant hunts whenever
possible and he took his Lakeland terriers with him, using them
whenever invited to do so. He would also remove problem foxes for

Willie (3rd from left) enjoying a day out with the Colne Valley beagles.

any farmers, or keepers, who asked him, especially if the hunt could not attend to the problem. His Lakeland terriers continued game and George Newcombe took up breeding this strain and used them to great effect both privately and with several North Yorkshire mounted hunts, as well as with one or two fell packs. Willie remained secretary of the International Hound Trail Committee, however, maintaining his links with the sport and he was also sometime secretary of the Loweswater Agricultural Society.

Billy Wilkinson's cartoon of Willie Irving.

CHAPTER 18

The End of an Era

Willie Irving was one of the Ennerdale-bred lads who were hard-schooled in hunting with hounds, with terriers and in other Lakeland traditions. He was successful at everything he turned his hand to, simply because he was determined and hardworking. He established the Melbreak as one of the leading fell packs of his day and made a massive contribution to the Lakeland terrier scene, both registered and unregistered strains, to such an extent that he was asked to judge at Crufts in 1968, which, sadly, wasn't to be. All of the fell pack Huntsmen were proud to have Jim Fleming terriers serving at their hunt and Fleming's stock was based on Irving's wonderful looker and worker, Turk.

A whole host of noted breeders can all trace their dogs back to Willie's Turk of Melbreak including John Cowen, Graham Ward, Cyril Breay and Frank Buck (they used Tear 'Em and a son of this dog to bring into their strain. Tear 'Em was a son of Myrt and thus a great grandson of Irving's Turk. They also used Hardisty's Turk on their bitches), Cyril Tyson, Gary Middleton, Sid Wilkinson, Anthony Barker, Max Buck, Maurice Bell and Brian Nuttall.

All modern bloodlines owe at least some of their heritage to the game earth dogs belonging to Willie Irving. George Ridley, former Huntsman of the North Lonsdale Foxhounds, once Whipped-in to Harry Hardisty and he used Irving-bred terriers too, as did Walt Parkin of the Lunesdale. His stock was partly bred from Irving Lakeland terriers. Jorrocks, registered as Border Raider, as seen in the 1956 photo out with the Blencathra, was considered by Willie to be the best type he had bred and this dog saw service at the Melbreak before Willie retired. Willie was also used to promote John Peel Ale by the Workington Brewery Company and he dressed up as John

Peel and attended different functions where the press gave them much publicity.

Willie developed a type of bone cancer and became seriously ill. A specialist was sent for by his doctor and he was visited at his home in Cockermouth. It was decided to send him to hospital at Whitehaven and it was here that he sadly passed away two weeks later, on November 26th 1966.

The funeral service was held at Lorton church and the tributes poured in. The obituaries are moving and give some indication of his widespread popularity and they extol him as an honest and reliable man. He was remembered for his kindness and as someone who always made certain that youngsters got about safely when out hunting, despite the fact that, as a Huntsman he had to try to keep with his hounds.

Included in these tributes were hunting songs written especially for him and these celebrate a rich and full life. He was survived by his wife, Maud, and two daughters Maud and Pearl, as well as grandchildren. Maud continued to live at Prospect House for some time, but then moved back to Lorton for her final years. She died on November 26th 1979, exactly thirteen years to the day her husband had passed away.

The Willie Irving Memorial Trophy, an award still presented each year to the best champion hound at the Cockermouth Show.

Hunting Songs Written in Tribute

The following appeared shortly after Willie's death in 1966:

The Late Willie Irving: In Memoriam

Bleak blows the breeze o'er the crest of steep Melbreak
Here are the woodland where oft' times he roved.
Wave upon wave flow the fronds of the fell–brake
But our friend, he is gone from the scenes he once loved.
Now, nought of sadness or care can befall him.
He from world conflict has now 'gone away'.
Only in mem'ry our hearts may recall him
Where the lights of 'Kirksteel' mark the closing of day.
Friendship in friends is past all earthly measure
Craving not glory for self, nor renown.
So with hearts meekly humble his name we will treasure
Until for us also, life's mists hasten down.
Bleak blows the breeze o'er the crest of steep Melbreak
And the horn of the hunter still brooks no delay.
Up hill and down hollow, by scree and thro' fell–brake
Let us follow his footsteps, "Hark forrard, away."

D.P.

Gone Far Away

Now here's a song of Will Irving,
A Huntsman you all loved so well.
No more his voice will be calling
O'er mountain, o'er crag and o'er dell.

Chorus:
Far away, far away,
From Melbreak's broad bosom away.
The church bell tolls o'er the valley,
For he's gone far, far away.

A man o' the fells was Will Irving.
Honest and true was his way.
Happy and smiling at morning
A greeting for hunters all gay.

All his life he travelled the hillside.
He gave of his best for the sport.
Kindness and friendship was always
His theme for those that he taught.

And long we'll remember Will Irving
And bless the day he was born.
May his memory be blessed by all sportsmen.
When they meet on a fine hunting morn.

William Hill, 1966

Oregill Copper Coin

It has long been believed that Alf Johnston bred the terrier Oregill Copper Coin, but according to Alf's son, the father of Alan Johnston who continues to breed the Oregill strain of Lakeland terrier, it was a chap called Fearon who bred this dog. The pedigree backs this up as Merry Faun, or Merry Foam (it is not clear which name is correct, though other pedigrees support Merry Faun), was not of the Oregill kennels, though she was bred out of Oregill Lakelands and was probably purchased by Fearon as a puppy.

This bitch then served at the Melbreak because Fearon, probably Dan, or Steve, was a regular and keen supporter and it was he who actually bred Copper Coin, using Oregill Cracker as stud to his bitch. It seems Alf then purchased back Jack (his 'pet' name for Copper Coin) as a young adult dog, from Fearon, probably because the dog was a terror and a confirmed cat killer.

It is said that Jack never saw a fox, but I believe Fearon did enter him at the Melbreak, and subsequently sold him because he didn't get on with either hound or terrier (he walked hounds for the Melbreak and had his own team of terriers). Why would such notables as Willie, Harry, Arthur Irving and Frank Pepper use this dog on their bitches if they hadn't shown his worth at fox? Willie, in fact, used him on at least three occasions, beginning in 1949 when Jack was about one year old (many Lakelands were entered to fox as early as nine months of age in those days). They didn't use non-workers and only proven stud dogs and brood bitches were allowed to produce offspring.

I am certain that Copper Coin did see some work at fox before he began the rounds at Kennel Club shows. Oregill Cracker also showed great working instinct and he may well have seen a fox or two at some time, possibly after he had become a champion. Alan recalls a tale told him by his father, of a time when Alf discovered a rat at the kennels. Oregill Cracker ('pet' name Grip) was fetched from his run and he slew the rat quickly and eagerly. Many of the Oregill-strain Lakelands displayed a keen working instinct and many did see some service at the Melbreak, as early LTA members were chiefly concerned with maintaining working qualities, as well as good type.

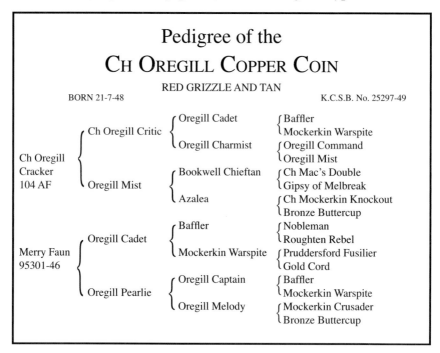

Pedigree of the
CH OREGILL COPPER COIN
RED GRIZZLE AND TAN
BORN 21-7-48   K.C.S.B. No. 25297-49

		Oregill Cadet	Baffler
	Ch Oregill Critic		Mockerkin Warspite
Ch Oregill		Oregill Charmist	Oregill Command
Cracker			Oregill Mist
104 AF	Oregill Mist	Bookwell Chieftan	Ch Mac's Double
			Gipsy of Melbreak
		Azalea	Ch Mockerkin Knockout
			Bronze Buttercup
		Baffler	Nobleman
	Oregill Cadet		Roughten Rebel
Merry Faun		Mockerkin Warspite	Pruddersford Fusilier
95301-46			Gold Cord
		Oregill Captain	Baffler
	Oregill Pearlie		Mockerkin Warspite
		Oregill Melody	Mockerkin Crusader
			Bronze Buttercup

An advertisement for John Peel Export Ale in which the model for the quintessential Huntsman is Willie Irving.

The Breeding of some of Willie Irving's terriers

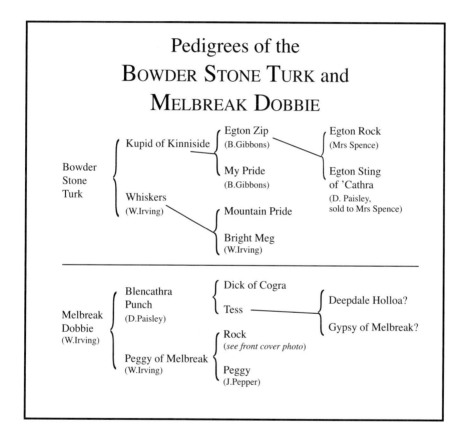

Pedigrees of the
BOWDER STONE TURK and
MELBREAK DOBBIE

Bowder Stone Turk
- Kupid of Kinniside
  - Egton Zip (B.Gibbons)
    - Egton Rock (Mrs Spence)
  - My Pride (B.Gibbons)
    - Egton Sting of 'Cathra (D. Paisley, sold to Mrs Spence)
- Whiskers (W.Irving)
  - Mountain Pride
  - Bright Meg (W.Irving)

Melbreak Dobbie (W.Irving)
- Blencathra Punch (D.Paisley)
  - Dick of Cogra
  - Tess
    - Deepdale Holloa?
    - Gypsy of Melbreak?
- Peggy of Melbreak (W.Irving)
  - Rock (*see front cover photo*)
  - Peggy (J.Pepper)

Pedigree of
MICK OF MILLAR PLACE

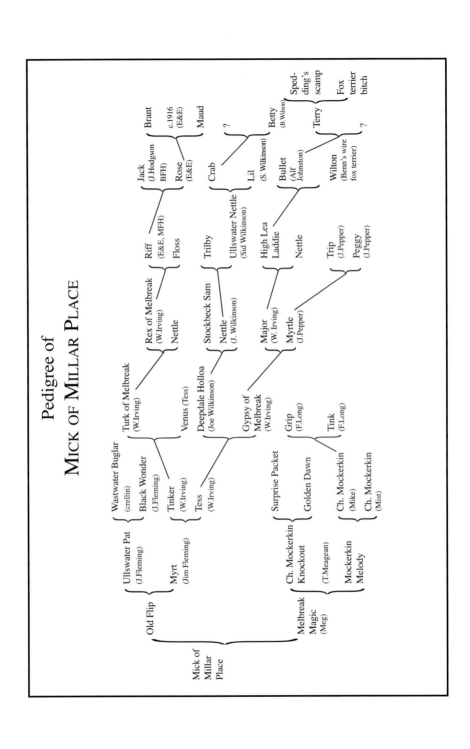

Pedigree of JUDY, TEAR 'EM, JIM

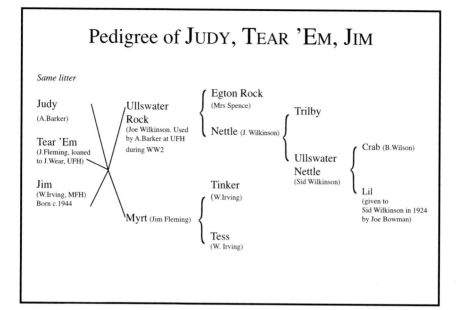

Same litter

Judy (A.Barker)

Tear 'Em (J.Fleming, loaned to J.Wear, UFH)

Jim (W.Irving, MFH) Born c.1944

Ullswater Rock (Joe Wilkinson. Used by A.Barker at UFH during WW2)
- Egton Rock (Mrs Spence)
- Nettle (J. Wilkinson)
  - Trilby
    - Ullswater Nettle (Sid Wilkinson)
      - Crab (B.Wilson)
      - Lil (given to Sid Wilkinson in 1924 by Joe Bowman)

Myrt (Jim Fleming)
- Tinker (W.Irving)
- Tess (W. Irving)

Pedigree of ROCK

(Sid Wilkinson)

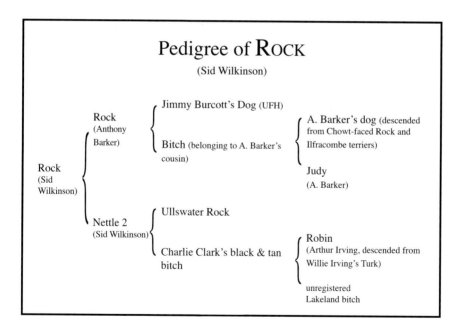

Rock (Sid Wilkinson)

Rock (Anthony Barker)
- Jimmy Burcott's Dog (UFH)
- Bitch (belonging to A. Barker's cousin)
  - A. Barker's dog (descended from Chowt-faced Rock and Ilfracombe terriers)
  - Judy (A. Barker)

Nettle 2 (Sid Wilkinson)
- Ullswater Rock
- Charlie Clark's black & tan bitch
  - Robin (Arthur Irving, descended from Willie Irving's Turk)
  - unregistered Lakeland bitch

The Breeding of some Melbreak Hounds
(supplied by Gordon Bland)

Pedigree of the
MELBREAK FOXHOUNDS

Born 08.06.28   Entered 1929

Parents	Grand-parents	Great Grand-parents	G-G-Grand-parents	G-G-G-G-ps
		Sire { Sire / Dam		
	Sire {	Dam { Sire / Dam		
Sire: Ullswater Major {		Sire { Sire / Dam		
	Dam {	Dam { Sire / Dam		

Cracker and Cora

Dam: Crafty 22 {	Sire: Ullswater Cracker {	Sire: Ullswater Matchless {	Sire: Ullswater Dingler / Dam: Ullswater Melody
		Dam { Sire / Dam	
	Dam: Rival 17 {	Sire: Royal {	Sire: Ragman / Dam: Merry — Sweeper / Melody
		Dam: Ullswater Brockless {	Sire / Dam

Pedigree of the
MELBREAK FOXHOUNDS

Born 1933   Entered 1934

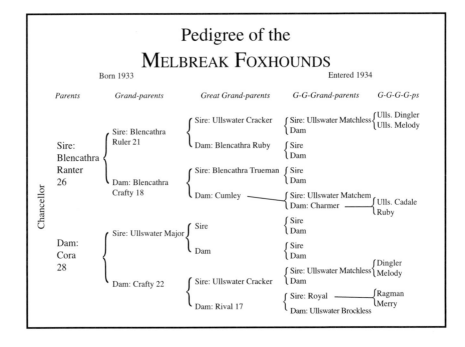

Chancellor

Parents	Grand-parents	Great Grand-parents	G-G-Grand-parents	G-G-G-G-ps
Sire: Blencathra Ranter 26 {	Sire: Blencathra Ruler 21 {	Sire: Ullswater Cracker {	Sire: Ullswater Matchless { Ulls. Dingler / Ulls. Melody	
		Dam: Blencathra Ruby {	Sire / Dam	
	Dam: Blencathra Crafty 18 {	Sire: Blencathra Trueman {	Sire / Dam	
		Dam: Cumley — {	Sire: Ullswater Matchem / Dam: Charmer — Ulls. Cadale / Ruby	
Dam: Cora 28 {	Sire: Ullswater Major {	Sire {	Sire / Dam	
		Dam {	Sire / Dam	
	Dam: Crafty 22 {	Sire: Ullswater Cracker {	Sire: Ullswater Matchless { Dingler / Melody / Dam	
		Dam: Rival 17 {	Sire: Royal — Ragman / Merry / Dam: Ullswater Brockless	

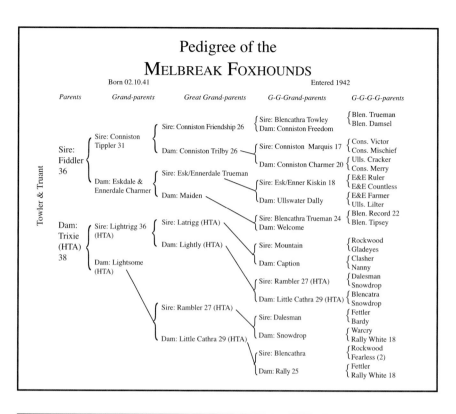

Pedigree of the
MELBREAK FOXHOUNDS

Born 02.10.41   Entered 1942

Towler & Truant

Parents	Grand-parents	Great Grand-parents	G-G-Grand-parents	G-G-G-G-parents

Sire: Fiddler 36

- Sire: Conniston Tippler 31
  - Sire: Conniston Friendship 26
    - Sire: Blencathra Towley — Blen. Trueman / Blen. Damsel
    - Dam: Conniston Freedom
  - Dam: Conniston Trilby 26
    - Sire: Conniston Marquis 17 — Cons. Victor / Cons. Mischief
    - Dam: Conniston Charmer 20 — Ulls. Cracker / Cons. Merry
- Dam: Eskdale & Ennerdale Charmer
  - Sire: Esk/Ennerdale Trueman
    - Sire: Esk/Enner Kiskin 18 — E&E Ruler / E&E Countless
  - Dam: Maiden
    - Dam: Ullswater Dally — E&E Farmer / Ulls. Lilter

Dam: Trixie (HTA) 38

- Sire: Lightrigg 36 (HTA)
  - Sire: Latrigg (HTA)
    - Sire: Blencathra Trueman 24 — Blen. Record 22 / Blen. Tipsey
    - Dam: Welcome
  - Dam: Lightly (HTA)
    - Sire: Mountain — Rockwood / Gladeyes
    - Dam: Caption — Clasher / Nanny
- Dam: Lightsome (HTA)
  - Sire: Rambler 27 (HTA)
    - Sire: Rambler 27 (HTA) — Dalesman / Snowdrop
    - Dam: Little Cathra 29 (HTA) — Blencatra / Snowdrop
  - Dam: Little Cathra 29 (HTA)
    - Sire: Dalesman — Fettler / Bardy
    - Dam: Snowdrop — Warcry / Rally White 18
    - Sire: Blencathra — Rockwood / Fearless (2)
    - Dam: Rally 25 — Fettler / Rally White 18

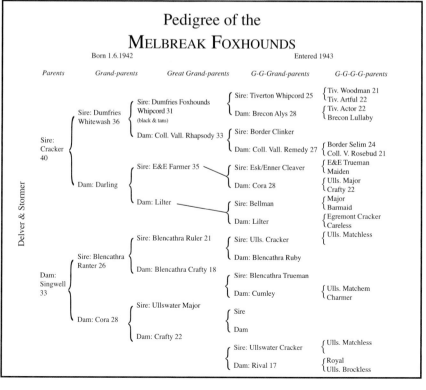

Pedigree of the
MELBREAK FOXHOUNDS

Born 1.6.1942   Entered 1943

Delver & Stormer

Parents	Grand-parents	Great Grand-parents	G-G-Grand-parents	G-G-G-G-parents

Sire: Cracker 40

- Sire: Dumfries Whitewash 36
  - Sire: Dumfries Foxhounds Whipcord 31 (black & tans)
    - Sire: Tiverton Whipcord 25 — Tiv. Woodman 21 / Tiv. Artful 22
    - Dam: Brecon Alys 28 — Tiv. Actor 22 / Brecon Lullaby
  - Dam: Coll. Vall. Rhapsody 33
    - Sire: Border Clinker
    - Dam: Coll. Vall. Remedy 27 — Border Selim 24 / Coll. V. Rosebud 21
- Dam: Darling
  - Sire: E&E Farmer 35
    - Sire: Esk/Enner Cleaver — E&E Trueman / Maiden
    - Dam: Cora 28 — Ulls. Major / Crafty 22
  - Dam: Lilter
    - Sire: Bellman — Major / Barmaid
    - Dam: Lilter — Egremont Cracker / Careless

Dam: Singwell 33

- Sire: Blencathra Ranter 26
  - Sire: Blencathra Ruler 21
    - Sire: Ulls. Cracker — Ulls. Matchless
    - Dam: Blencathra Ruby
  - Dam: Blencathra Crafty 18
    - Sire: Blencathra Trueman
    - Dam: Cumley — Ulls. Matchem / Charmer
- Dam: Cora 28
  - Sire: Ullswater Major
    - Sire
    - Dam
  - Dam: Crafty 22
    - Sire: Ullswater Cracker — Ulls. Matchless
    - Dam: Rival 17 — Royal / Ulls. Brockless

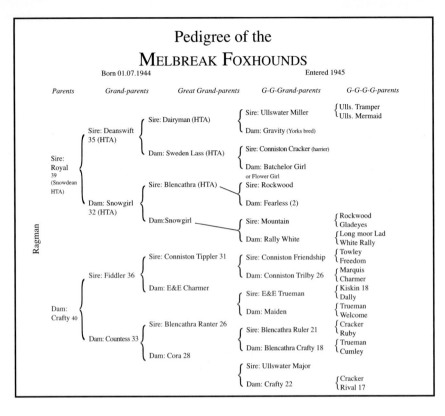

Pedigree of the
MELBREAK FOXHOUNDS

Born 01.07.1944   Entered 1945

Parents   *Grand-parents*   *Great Grand-parents*   *G-G-Grand-parents*   *G-G-G-parents*

Ragman

Sire: Royal 39 (Snowdean HTA)

Sire: Deanswift 35 (HTA)
- Sire: Dairyman (HTA)
  - Sire: Ullswater Miller
    - Ulls. Tramper
    - Ulls. Mermaid
  - Dam: Gravity (Yorks bred)
- Dam: Sweden Lass (HTA)
  - Sire: Conniston Cracker (harrier)
  - Dam: Batchelor Girl or Flower Girl

Dam: Snowgirl 32 (HTA)
- Sire: Blencathra (HTA)
  - Sire: Rockwood
  - Dam: Fearless (2)
- Dam: Snowgirl
  - Sire: Mountain
    - Rockwood
    - Gladeyes
  - Dam: Rally White
    - Long moor Lad
    - White Rally

Dam: Crafty 40

Sire: Fiddler 36
- Sire: Conniston Tippler 31
  - Sire: Conniston Friendship
    - Towley
    - Freedom
  - Dam: Conniston Trilby 26
    - Marquis
    - Charmer
- Dam: E&E Charmer
  - Sire: E&E Trueman
    - Kiskin 18
    - Dally
  - Dam: Maiden
    - Trueman
    - Welcome

Dam: Countess 33
- Sire: Blencathra Ranter 26
  - Sire: Blencathra Ruler 21
    - Cracker
    - Ruby
  - Dam: Blencathra Crafty 18
    - Trueman
    - Cumley
- Dam: Cora 28
  - Sire: Ullswater Major
  - Dam: Crafty 22
    - Cracker
    - Rival 17

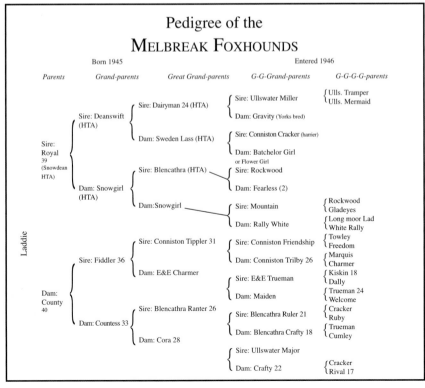

Pedigree of the
MELBREAK FOXHOUNDS

Born 1945   Entered 1946

Parents   *Grand-parents*   *Great Grand-parents*   *G-G-Grand-parents*   *G-G-G-parents*

Laddie

Sire: Royal 39 (Snowdean HTA)

Sire: Deanswift (HTA)
- Sire: Dairyman 24 (HTA)
  - Sire: Ullswater Miller
    - Ulls. Tramper
    - Ulls. Mermaid
  - Dam: Gravity (Yorks bred)
- Dam: Sweden Lass (HTA)
  - Sire: Conniston Cracker (harrier)
  - Dam: Batchelor Girl or Flower Girl

Dam: Snowgirl (HTA)
- Sire: Blencathra (HTA)
  - Sire: Rockwood
  - Dam: Fearless (2)
- Dam: Snowgirl
  - Sire: Mountain
    - Rockwood
    - Gladeyes
  - Dam: Rally White
    - Long moor Lad
    - White Rally

Dam: County 40

Sire: Fiddler 36
- Sire: Conniston Tippler 31
  - Sire: Conniston Friendship
    - Towley
    - Freedom
  - Dam: Conniston Trilby 26
    - Marquis
    - Charmer
- Dam: E&E Charmer
  - Sire: E&E Trueman
    - Kiskin 18
    - Dally
  - Dam: Maiden
    - Trueman 24
    - Welcome

Dam: Countess 33
- Sire: Blencathra Ranter 26
  - Sire: Blencathra Ruler 21
    - Cracker
    - Ruby
  - Dam: Blencathra Crafty 18
    - Trueman
    - Cumley
- Dam: Cora 28
  - Sire: Ullswater Major
  - Dam: Crafty 22
    - Cracker
    - Rival 17

More Information on Terrier Breeding

Pearl Wilson recently rediscovered two old notebooks that belonged to her father, Willie Irving, and these shed much new light on the breeding of Irving's stock and the way in which he operated as Huntsman of the Melbreak. Amongst these notes was an old letter that tells how Irving's Rex of Melbreak was bred, though we do not know the author of the letter, as it certainly wasn't Willie Irving. Rex was sired by Riff, that we already know, and Riff was born in 1918 and served first at the Eskdale and Ennerdale, then at the Melbreak after 1926. The sire of Riff was Jack, owned by J.W. Hodgson, the Blencathra Whipper-in from 1913–1915, and it is the breeding of this terrier, previously unknown, which concerns us.

Jack was actually bred by Fred Bartle of Caldbeck (a friend of Douglas Paisley and one who often used Paisley's stud dogs on his bitches) and he was sired by Blencathra Turk, out of Bartle's Meg, though the letter doesn't state who owned this stud dog. Could this be Dalton's famous Turk, considered the Patriarch of all registered and unregistered Lakelands? Or, could this dog have been one of Paisley's terriers? It is said that Dalton's Turk was sired by Gillert, a Cockermouth Otterhounds terrier, though this scanty reference I found could well be wrong. My money would be on this Blencathra Turk being Dalton's famous dog (the timing coincides exactly with when Turk was around and rapidly becoming a legend throughout the fell country). Like all fell pack Huntsmen, Dalton walked many of his terriers with keen followers and this old letter states that Riff, either belonging to, or walked with, Sid McNichol, sired Turk. He in turn was bred out of Alan Nelson's Dobbie, which died whilst at work with the Melbreak (Alan Nelson's stock went back to Willie Tyson's and Will Ritson's terrier strains, though it was influenced by Irving's terriers after 1926).

The dam of this Turk was a Blencathra bitch, Span, which had been named after Long Span, the Waterloo Cup winner, which was walked with R. Graves. The dam of Riff, the sire of Turk, was Fan, another Blencathra bitch walked by G. Bainbridge of the Nags Head at Thirlmere; an Inn that was lost when the water level was increased in order to supply drinking water to an increasing British population. Poor Turk was loaned to the Eskdale and Ennerdale Hunt by Dalton and it was there that he met his death, whilst working fox at Pillar Ghyll, Ennerdale. If this Turk was indeed Dalton's famous worker and looker, then Irving's stock is directly linked to him via Rex and, of course, his son, Turk of Melbreak.

Willie's old notebooks tell us that Maud, the dam of Rose (the mother of both Willie Porter's Riff of 1918 and Irving's Felix) was, in fact, a white Irish terrier. It has long been speculated that Irish terrier stock had been used to infuse Fell and Lakeland strains and here we have definite written proof. Maud was out of Irish terrier stock and Willie obtained this bitch in 1916 when he first began keeping his own team of terriers. The notes also tell us that Mac, the sire of Felix, belonged to Peter Long and it is known that his strain was descended from Dalton's Turk. Mac was a grandson of Blencathra Rock and Vic and one can be certain that at least one of these terriers would be out of Turk. All of Dalton's stock, in fact, as well as most terriers in the Lake District after this time, were descended from Dalton's famous working terrier, Turk.

These notes also record the breeding of Nettle, the dam of Turk of Melbreak, and she was sired by Salt, out of Furious Cracksman and Maisie, two early Lakeland's that feature in several pedigrees, and her dam was Oracle, out of Barmie Brigadier and Buckabout Betty. The dam of Majore, Nettle, previously thought to have been the same dam that gave birth to Turk of Melbreak, was, in fact, a different bitch and she was out of Rock and Tiny. Rock was out of Crab and Meg and Tiny was out of Grip and Floss. Irving also records that High Lea Laddie was sired by Terry, out of Oregill Lady. Terry was out of Scamp and Betty, the stud belonging to Spedding and the bitch belonging to Mawson. Betty was a wire fox terrier. Oregill Lady was out of Tinker and Vic of Wastwater. This is not in agreement with Alf Johnston's account of the breeding of this dog, but I would not dismiss Irving's account as Terry actually served at the Melbreak and may well have belonged to him (also, Irving recorded these notes at the time when High Lea Laddie was standing at stud, whilst Alf Johnston wrote of the breeding of this dog decades after the event, so it is possible his memory had failed him). Terry was walked at the Swinburn farm according to Irving's notes, which indicates that he did indeed own this dog and used it on Alf's bitch to breed High Lea Laddie. Kim, the sire of Red Lady, a bitch terrier Alf Johnston stated had introduced much aggression into pedigree Lakeland bloodlines, was a brother to High Lea Laddie, but he was only aggressive if not given enough work. Red Lady was the dam of Champion Mockerkin Mac, when put to Mockerkin Mike.

Willie also noted the breeding of Stockbeck Sam, the sire of Deepdale Holloa, who, Irving's notes tell us, was actually Rock, the leggy Lakeland at Irving's feet in his famous Crummock Water photo found on the cover of this book. I thought this dog may well have been bred by Bob Gibbons and, indeed, a Rock bred by him did serve at the Melbreak and was walked with a Mr Cameron who was a farm worker at the Cannon farm, Darling How, from 1934 until 1941 when the dog seems to have retired (this Rock was possibly Kupid of Kinniside). He was grizzle in colour, whilst Deepdale Holloa, the Rock in the photo, was clearly black and tan. Stockbeck Sam was out of Blencathra Boy and Ribston Pippin, being bred the same way as Albermarle Pippin, the dam of Champion Evergreen's Double. Blencathra Boy was bred out of a long line of Blencathra Hunt terriers and was descended from Dalton's Turk, whilst Ribston Pippin, Irving's notes confirm, was out of a long line of Coniston Hunt terriers.

Pippin was sired by Crab, a famous Coniston terrier owned by Anthony Chapman, the father of George, and her dam was Mettle, not Nettle as previously thought. Crab was sired by Rock, a Rochdale Hunt terrier (this pack hunted hares and foxes), out of Pym of the Coniston. Mettle was out of Coniston Squib and Metz. It is interesting to note that all of the fell packs played a major role in establishing the early pedigree Lakeland. Coniston Squib may well be the same terrier that served at the Melbreak and was walked by Cecil Studholme of Whitehaven.

A list for the 1940/41 season tells us that Irving's Meg was out of Tinker and Mist. Punch was out of Tinker and Tess and was undoubtedly a brother of Fleming's Myrt. Judy, another famous Irving Lakeland, was out of Whisk and Tess. Gyp was out of Majore and Nan and Rusty was out of the Bob Gibbons bred Rock and Smile. Jen was out of Ronnie Porter's Tinker and Moore's Vic. One of the Peggy's was out of Mowdy Robinson's Rufus and Dart, a bitch bred out of Rock and Nip. Misty was also out of Rock and Nip. Squick was walked by Hamilton Dougherty and another Peggy was out of Mac and Teaser. This teaser was bred out of Turk and Teaser. Peggy was walked at Gatesgarth by Miss Nelson. There was another Peggy out of Nigger and Maud walked by Frank Coates.

Willie left the list of his terriers for all seasons at the hunt, but the 1926 list is fascinating, as several of these terriers laid the foundation for the pedigree Lakeland. Boss, Tinker, Sting, Trig, Squib, Riff, Midge, Grip, Peggy, Felix, Rose, Floss and Blue Floss, Bill, Twig, Tim, another Grip, and Crab. These were all available for Irving's use when he started as Huntsman and several were brought with him from the Eskdale and Ennerdale, while others were still at walk from when the previous Huntsman held the reins, being bred out of famous old Melbreak lines that were winning shows all across the Lake District. Others belonged to local farmers.

After 1926, however, Willie records several puppies that he bred and put out at walk, or supplied to local farmers and villagers. He also tells us that Boss later died of injuries to his back whilst flushing a fox from a crag on Whiteside. Sandy, the Grandsire of Thomas Rawlings Gillert, the sire of Sheik, the dog registered by Bob Gibbons in 1933, served with the Melbreak and was either walked, or owned, by Hamilton Dougherty. This terrier also served with the Eskdale and Ennerdale and was with the Melbreak by 1928.

In 1929 Irving produced pups out of Bruce and Felix, supplying, among others, Cecil Studholme and Fletcher with walks, and Rex and Squib, with two of these pups going out at walk. Bruce, sadly, was lost to ground on Haystacks that season. Tinker was lost to ground at Buttermere and Irving sent Spike, Jock and Titch to serve with Otterhounds, though he doesn't state which pack. It seems he supplied several hunts with terriers, including the Rochdale Hunt mentioned previously.

Willie had terriers out at walk as far away as Workington and Wasdale. Peggy and Mist were also sent to serve with Otterhounds. There is no date given for this, but it seems it was the very early 1930s. J. Norman, Jim Kitchen, Mowdy Robinson, J. Bland of Wasdale and Cecil Studholme of Whitehaven were regular terrier walkers, as were Bruce and Moore. The 1931/32 season saw Peggy, Judy, Turk and Tiny in kennels with Irving, but the rest were out at walk, including another bitch, white Peggy, that was with Jim Kitchen. This was probably the same Peggy that was also sent to serve with Otterhounds. This Peggy had no doubt inherited her colouring from the white Irish terrier, Maud. Nit was walked by Mowdy Robinson. During the 1943/44 season Monty arrived on loan from Jim Fleming of Grasmere and Willie put him at walk at Corn How, with a Mr W. Hope. Monty died the following season while still on loan, though Willie doesn't state how.

In 1943 he sold Rufus to Rochdale, probably to the Rochdale Hunt, though this is not conclusive. That same year Meg died whelping and Buffer and Sting also died whilst at work. These records also show that several terriers were walked with the Hardisty family, including Sid and Harry, long before Harry became Whipper-in, though they may also have owned some of these terriers.

The confusing problem is that hounds and terriers were traditionally referred to as belonging to those who walked them, despite the fact that they were really the property of the hunt and the breeding programmes were implemented, or at least overseen, by the Huntsman. Willie also notes that he swapped and sold terriers to Joe Armstrong, one being Major, and took one or two on loan from Joe at times. Pearl states that Joe bred some wonderfully game terriers and it is clear from these notes that his strain contained quite a number of Irving's dogs in their pedigrees.

These notes are a wonderful find that record much more than I have been able to put down here, including much of the breeding of very early Lakeland terrier stock. They also prove that Willie Irving played a major role in those early breeding programmes and continued to do so throughout his long and eventful life. For instance, Mick and Trim, bred down from the Turk line, became the top-winning terriers of the 1940s and early 50s and they literally won everywhere, even outside the Lake District, being almost unbeatable.

Trim produced 21 puppies in just one year, her offspring were so popular, and Mick served many, many bitches. This pair were also grand workers and Harry Irving produced much of his stock out of Mick and Trim, and no doubt Arthur used some of their offspring at the Eskdale and Ennerdale Hunt too.

Pearl can remember a hunt in the Loweswater area that was halted by Reynard going to ground at Grange, Loweswater. This was a long drain that wasn't easy to work and Irving was a little hesitant about putting in his top dog. However, he entered Mick and the dog scrambled along this huge earth for 100 yards or more and caught up with his fox, which bolted soon after. Mick was extensively used with hounds and was very battle-scarred. Most working Lakeland terriers of today can be traced back to one or other of this famous pair of Melbreak earth dogs.